Tip

of the

Spear

For Love of Thy Country

Bob W. Cannady

While the contents of this book are based on actual events, names, locations, certain details, and other pertinent facts have been changed or altered to protect any and all proprietary information.

Dedication

To all the military servicemen and women from the past, the present, and future who have engaged in horrific events for their country. I dedicate this book to all of you, my brothers and sisters.

May God protect and watch out for you all in your time of need.

————————————————————————→

Acknowledgments

I would like to extend my personal thanks and gratitude to Chester L. Dosher.

Thanks for being my close friend and for helping me with my book through editing and counseling. Thank you also for being there when I needed someone to talk to.

Contents

Foreword

Many recognize the iconic relic that graces the cover of this book — the Spear of Destiny, the lance head used by a Roman Centurion named Longinus to pierce the side of Christ as he hung on the cross. The Crusaders were said to have carried it on a standard at the head of their army. Attila the Hun was rumored to have attained the lance as he cut his way across Europe. Stories of the power of the Holy Lance span centuries, and over the years, men of great power have been associated with it.

Successful military leaders, including Theodosius, Alaric, Charles Martel, Charlemagne, and Frederick Barbarossa were all alleged to have held the lance. According to legend, Charlemagne carried the lance through 47 battles, but died when he accidently dropped it. Barbarossa died only a few minutes after the lance slipped out of his hands while crossing a stream. Napoleon believed the legend and attempted to gain control of the lance after the battle of Austerlitz, but it had been smuggled out of Vienna prior to the battle. He never attained it. Hitler took possession of the lance from the Hofburg Museum after declaring Austria part of the Third Reich.

The lance and its legend came to be associated with power — specifically, the power of the spear's possessor to rule the world. Oddly, none who held the spear attained the ultimate power and domination that they sought. Only Longinus, the lance's first owner, ever attained anything of ultimate value from association with the Holy Lance. Longinus, the Roman Centurion assigned to preside over Christ's crucifixion, was nearly blind. His failing eyesight might have been reason for his assignment to the duties of executions, since he would not have been seen fit for regular military service. Upon piercing Christ's side, blood from the wound splashed into Longinus' eyes and his sight was fully restored. Longinus remarked, "Indeed, this was the Son of God!" [Mark 15:39]. He left the military and converted. He went on to become Saint Longinus.

Perhaps only a soldier can know true peace, for all he has known is war. As I mentioned previously, those that sought power in possessing the Holy Lance never achieved it. For Longinus, an instrument of war became the key to salvation. The realization and acceptance of God helps put war's horrors in perspective and allows the soldier the peace he has fought so hard for. Our faith and God's forgiveness offers us the same salvation received by Longinus. Consider the lance in any manner you wish. For me, I prefer Longinus' view.

Introduction

My dad died just prior to my birth. My mother, a single parent, struggled to raise two growing boys with no help. She was completely on her own. We grew up in Montana, and amid this natural splendor, she raised her two boys and struggled through life, marrying man after man to help keep food on the table and a roof over our heads. As these men came and went from our lives, it was always the same scenario; the vicious cycle of an abusive relationship for my mother, my brother, and I. Mom would live with each as long as she could, divorce them, and move on.

Growing up poor, I was teased and ridiculed by the other children at school. A teacher once told me that I would never amount to anything, and I spent the rest of my life attempting to discard that label. I *could* be successful. I *wanted* to succeed, to have others proud of me. I *wanted* to be special. I didn't realize that all that really mattered was my mother's opinion. In her eyes, I had always been special. Mom finally met a kind and gentle man that helped us through the hard times, but for me, life began with the Marines.

I spent five years as a Marine reconnaissance sniper and three years in the Army Special Forces. During my years in special operations, I found hidden in the walls of America things that no one should know — or should want to know. I will talk about some of these personal experiences, as well as some of my colleagues. Although some of these missions are still classified, I will change some content and names to protect both confidentiality and myself. The events of which I write are horrific in nature, yet happen every day around the world. There is no media coverage of these events, no family members are aware of them, and most of all, they are never spoken of except among the few who participate in them.

Without special ops missions and the people who are willing to give their lives in their performance, this nation would not exist. Although easy to dismiss when surrounded by the freedom, security, and convenience that is American society, not every country possesses such luxuries. In this county, we are quick to judge and make our own assessments without all the facts. As an American, you have that right. I helped secure it for you.

In conveying my story to you, I will start at the beginning — where my life ended and where it began. I will end with two different countries, two different missions, and two different mindsets. I hope to impress upon the reader the person I was when I started, and the very different person I became. I hope this will shed new light and a new understanding of what the people behind the scenes endure in their service to their country — the people who, often unnoticed, ensure you will always have the freedoms you enjoy today.

The combat soldier is the lance thrust that decides the final outcome of any military campaign. Special operations are their eyes and ears. Whether their mission is reconnaissance or site specific targets, special operations provides the leading edge of ground troop entry. I dedicate this book to my close friends lost in Desert Storm and to the untold stories of their bravery and love of country. God bless them for their dedication and devotion to duty. This book is for them, their memory, and my own self-preservation. It is for those who are, those who were, and those who will someday be...the tip of the spear.

Chapter 1
Training — Making a Marine

Boys join the Marines. The Marines make them men. I don't know how many times I have heard the phrase "Marines are brainwashed." Being a former Marine, I can honestly say, yes we are. Is this a bad thing? You decide. The Marines teach discipline, pride, integrity, honesty, and honor. Finish what you start. Keep your hair trimmed. Press your uniform. Work from sunup to sundown. Listen to and obey your superiors. Love your country. Honor your parents. And most of all, build your self-esteem. If these are brainwashing techniques, maybe the rest of the world should try it. I love the Marines. I always will. If it weren't for their brainwashing, I wouldn't be the man that I am today. In fact, I might not even be alive.

Life in the military consisted of training and lots of specialty schools. Most of the special training schools are voluntary. You may quit at anytime. These are select schools for the best of the best. Although the training may seem cruel, you don't *have* to be there. As I said, you may quit at anytime — and most men do. Very few pass the special training schools. Most of the schools have a 60-80% dropout rate.

One of the first special training schools I attended was survival school in Bridgeport, California. It is largely for infantry Marines, but all Marines are eligible to attend. The school is designed to teach mountain survival. It was one week of learning to start fires, set snares, what vegetation to eat, fishing, building shelters, tracking, how to stay focused on living, and most importantly, not giving up. In survival situations, most causalities occur not from starvation, dehydration, or injury, but because people give up.

The first week, everything was great. We had instructors showing us all kinds of methods of fire-starting, setting snares, and everything you'd need to know in order to survive. It seemed so easy — until the time came to actually apply the techniques.

We were paired up and placed in 1,000-meter grid squares. Within the grid we had vegetation, water, and wildlife. We had a radio so we could check in for daily updates and in case of emergencies. We were given only the clothes on our backs, nothing else — no knife, nothing. Just you and your partner left in the forest attempting to survive for a week.

The first day out, we pretty much starved. We sat around and talked about food. We did our daily check-in and tried to make a shelter. Since the school was being held during the summer, we didn't fret the shelter too much, and we threw together a half-assed, ugly contraption. To punish our laziness, it started to rain. Needless to say, once the rain abated, we made immediate improvements. We started by finding big tree branches for the support beams, and utilized leafy plants for the roof. In about two hours, we had a nice shelter. We took some large rocks, smashed them together, and made some sharp digging utensils. We then dug out our shelter floor and made a trench around it so that rain would flow around it, not into it. Shelter made.

Initially, we ate watercress, a plant that grows in small creeks. It tasted like lettuce. It had no flavor and basically sucked. *I'm starving*. It was time to get serious and trap some food, but first we needed a fire. We gathered our materials and made a bow. The bow was made of a piece of wood found near our campsite, and we utilized our boot laces for a string.

Once we gathered our wood, it was time to put our skills to the test. We worked the bow for about an hour in an attempt to produce an ember. This method worked well in practice, when we had an instructor, but for some reason we were now having trouble with it. Finally, after about three hours, my partner succeeded in making a fire. All I produced was smoke and a lot of swear words.

With the fire made, we needed food. Using our boot laces and cut-up pieces of t-shirts, we made a set of snares. We set out the snares and waited. After two days of no success and losing 10 pounds, we realized that paying attention in class would have been beneficial. We had fire and shelter, but nothing to eat. I asked my buddy, "What do you think human tastes like?"

On the third day we caught a rabbit. We ate the entire rabbit, including cracking the bones and eating the marrow. That satisfied our hunger for a while. The next source of protein we turned to was worms. We ate a few during the remainder of the week, trying to keep up our strength. The week went by. I lost about 30 pounds, and my partner and I realized that we sucked at survival. Without doubt, we needed more training. Next time, I'd pay more attention to my instructors and not waste the opportunity.

Two years after the first survival school, I became a scout/sniper. I was paired with my buddy and spotter, Hodge. We were both fully adept in survival skills. I had met Hodge in Sniper School and we hit it off. We'd done everything together — gone through the same routines, the same training. Hodge and I had been back from Honduras about six months when we were scheduled for survival school. We had been through both the Recon Introduction Program (RIP) and Sniper School, and survival skills were taught extensively in both schools. This time surviving in the woods would be easy. This time around, the once hard school was going to be cakewalk.

I asked our Staff Sergeant who I would be paired with and what grid we were going in. He made a mistake — he trusted me. He told me I was paired with Hodge and we would go in on XYZ grid. Great! I put a plan in motion. I told Hodge he was with me, just like old times. This time, I didn't want to suffer during my week of survival testing. While everyone slept, we stocked up on Oreos, soda, chips, cookies, matches, ponchos, water, and all the food we could carry. We hauled all the contraband out to our grid and stashed it under a poncho, then snuck back into camp and waited on our orders. The orders came. Hodge and I were in ... oh no, not that grid with all the food! One thing the Marines taught me well was "overcome and adapt." I did. I cheated.

We were dropped off in our grid and we set up camp. Then Hodge and I sat under our poncho eating chips and dip and drinking Pepsi. The radio chatter started to come in. First it was some guy saying, "I just ate a worm," another saying, "I ate a snake." Hodge and I would reply that we were starving too, or, "We just ate a raw fish." This went on for the full week, with Hodge and me lying around gorging ourselves.

When everyone was picked up, Hodge and I were the only ones who had gained weight. When we arrived back to the base, everyone in the class ran for the PX. They came back devouring chips, cookies, and soda. The asked if we wanted any. We shook our heads and said no, we'd wait for dinner. The looks that followed were way too funny. They thought we were some bad dudes. In reality, we were just smarter. Hodge and I had the highest rating you could get in a survival class. We gave everyone advice on wilderness survival — we just left out the part about sneaking food into position prior to insertion. This went well until, late one night during a drinking session, we let our little secret slip. Not good. We all got a good laugh, but when the Staff Sergeant heard what happened, he tried to get us sent back up. Unsuccessful, he finally devised different ways to punish us. We were both on kitchen detail for weeks.

Our next school was very unique. It punished you in ways that I never knew imaginable. Before entry, you're sworn to secrecy because if details of this training were leaked, it would be easier to pass. Anyone who passes never tells the secrets — each individual has to discover them on his own. I can keep my oath by describing a few small details without giving too much away.

Imagine you are a POW, but not in some faraway camp — in your own backyard. I would say about 200 or so Marines start out. You're all shaved, stripped down to your underwear, put into bamboo cages, and starved. Damn starving schools — I hate them. For once I wish they'd have a school where they'd force you to eat.

You are surrounded by Orientals. They speak very little English and are there to torture you until you quit. All you have to do is say "I quit" or give up the mission you were assigned. It's that simple.

I was brought in while another Marine was coming out. He had been beaten to a pulp. Although this was in fact a school, once your are broken, once you have endured the mistreatment and abuse, you soon forgot you are in a school. I was immediately strapped to a hanging bar and the questioning started. I gave them the standard answers of name, rank, serial number. That wasn't quite good enough for the little slant-eyed bastards.

A side note here: Though I am not prejudiced toward any nationality, at the time, I did not see my "captors" as fellow Marines, even though they were, and were only doing their jobs. They were my abusers — they were the enemy. In order to train me thoroughly, and prepare me for the realities I might someday encounter, everything had to be as real as possible, hence the military's choice of assigning Oriental men to serve as our captors. Because of this reality, I soon felt like a real POW, and resented my captors and everything about them — hence, a temporary dislike for those who were abusing me emulated a temporary prejudice.

They started by slapping me in the mouth. Not enough. They took a bamboo rod and beat the back of my legs. I knew that this was a school and they were doing their jobs, but I made it my goal to beat their heads in if I saw them out and about when this was over.

On day four, I almost gave up when I saw what they were dragging out. It was a defibrillator machine. Electricity was not my friend. I was terrified of it. The main operative started by trying to be nice. He told me just give him a little info, then this machine didn't have to be used. I told him nothing. He turned on the defibrillator and I could hear it humming. He grabbed the paddles, and I was about shit myself. I tried to reason with him, telling him that he could actually stop my heart, but he just kept repeating, "Tell me why you are here." I told him nothing. He hit me with the paddles. I jumped about 10 feet. The funny thing was, there was just a little shock. Nothing like you see in the movies.

Oh, I see what's going on now! Head games. Now I definitely wasn't telling him shit. He reached over in front of me and turned the dial up, and the humming sound became louder. I took another look at the situation. The first time was just a test. Now the real thing was coming. I almost talked that time, but I soon found that the anticipation was way worse than the act. When he hit me with the paddles again, it was just a slightly more intense shock than the first one. ***Oh, it's your ass now!*** I realized that this was all a head game and now it was on. That didn't last long.

My big mouth has gotten me into trouble more than once in my lifetime. Now that I thought I had the game figured out, it did it again. I started to trash-talk them. Not good. I should have shut up and stopped calling them stupid gooks.

It was time for them to punish the big mouth. "Bring it on!" I said defiantly. Bad choice of words. They were smarter, and they were in charge! I was the idiot who never learns. There were some trenches out in the mud, each about 2 ½ feet deep, the bottom lined with rocks and mud. Over the top of each trench was a nice, electrified barbed wire fence. They locked my hands behind my back, put me on

6

my knees, and made me lean my head into the sidewall of the trench. Then they closed the wire gate across my back, and turned on the juice. One shock was enough and that was it — I sat obediently on my knees for two days in the mud, rocks, and water which lined the trench, not daring to rise for fear of another shock. I was given only a small cup of water and small cup of rice to eat.

On day three I was let out. I was broken, and kept my smart mouth shut. I was forced to crawl back to a bamboo cage. My knees were shot after being on the rocks for two days. I was a mess and in intense pain.

They put me in a 3' x 3' bamboo cage that was much too cramped for me. I sat there for three days. Each day they would give you cup of water and cup of rice. The lack of food and water wasn't as bad as the sleep deprivation. They had some little crap bastard that kept hitting me with a cattle prod to keep me awake. For three days I was afforded little food, water, or sleep, and was prodded like a cow. On the third day without sleep I was given my cup of rice. I gulped it down without looking, but something didn't seem right. I spat the rice back into the bowl only to find a bunch of maggots instead of rice. I was pissed. I cursed everyone in sight, swearing to kill each and every one. That cost me another day in the pen.

By this time, several people had dropped out. I didn't recognize any of them. We were constantly changing cages, being beaten and deprived of sleep. This was definitely an experience in psychological trauma. One cold and clammy night, the game moved up a notch. We had all lost a lot of weight, and the school seemed like it would never end. (By the way, this particular training doesn't have a set period of time. It only has a percentage of dropout rates, and then it ends.) We were about a month into it. They built a big fire and started up the barbeque pits. Then, to our surprise, they brought out about 30 pizzas. The smell was way too overwhelming. This little slant bastard came out and gave his speech to the cattle waiting for feed. "Gentlemen, you have all accomplished more than enough to be proud of, but now it's time to call it quits and go home. None of you should be ashamed. You have all gone so far. We are going to open up all the cages and you come out and have all the food and drink you like. Let's celebrate." Basically, he was saying if you come out, you're out of the program. We were all tired, hungry, and had had enough, but no one wanted to be the first one out the gate to give up. Unbeknownst to us, one of the instructors was in the program with us. We were led to believe he was just one of the guys. He led the pack, screaming he'd had enough and was going to eat. He was let out of the cage and he started eating. The herd of cattle followed. I would say we lost half the guys because of this one incident. Good tactics. After everyone who was going to leave left, they loaded them up in trucks and they were never seen again. As for the rest of us, we just sat there, smelled the food, and prayed for it all to be over.

When the day finally came, there were very few of us left. By now, I actually thought I *was* a POW. I had forgotten I was in a school — that's how traumatized I was. These people were very good at their jobs. The length of the school had been between two to three months. Out of 200 individuals, there were fewer than 30 left. Our hands were tied behind our backs and they put guns to our heads. We were marched out into the middle of a big field. We were put on our knees, guns still to our heads. I actually thought I was going to die. At that moment, a helicopter playing the "Star Spangled Banner" flew in. My heart soared and we all started to cry. It was a very emotional time for all of us. When it landed, a Major General walked out to us. We were untied and the slant eyes moved to the side. We stood at attention, as best we could. The General gave us a speech that will be ingrained in my head for the rest of my life. I wish I could share it with you all, but under oath, I can't. He pinned a badge on each of us and took us home. We were given a month off to recover.

The psychological trauma that we had endured was immense. Only a select few ever know what it's like — and this was nothing like what an actual POW goes through. This was just a little taste of it. I am sure what the wartime POWs actually go through is much worse, and lasts much longer. The only things that can keep you going are your family, friends, and your country. What else is there to live for? God loves the POWs. So do I. I hold them in high regard. I have wished many times that I could thank each one for what they have endured for this country.

In most training schools, they teach you how to deal with things like solitude, claustrophobia, and most of all, fear. After spending most of my military career in training schools, I was getting pretty good at all of them, but water survival school pushed me to the limits again. The lesson? What could happen if you fall out of a boat or helicopter and have to survive in the water by floating without life vest. Here you find out what it's like firsthand. In order to be admitted, you had to be an excellent swimmer.

For this training, I was taken into a building — a cement dungeon, no windows, totally black, with only one light at the bottom of a 10-foot-deep, 20' x 20' pool. A big fish bowl, that's the only way I can describe it. There was a camera with a little red light on the roof to watch you. The sides of the pool were concave. You couldn't grab on to them. There was a ladder on a winch, which was used to lower you down into the black abyss. Get the picture? Once again, I was given a little speech: "This pool is heated at a specific temperature. You will not become hypothermic. You will be placed in the pool, naked, for 24 hours to tread water. We will not come to get you until the 24 hours are up or you drown. Now is the time to quit. There is no quitting once you are placed in the water. That camera is watching you at all times. Do you wish to go in, or quit at this time?"

They lowered me into the pool and shut off the lights.

All I could see was the dim light on the bottom of the pool and the red light on the camera. After about two to four hours (I guess) I started to lose track of time — in fact, there was no way to judge time. I was getting tired and nervous. I worried I wasn't going to make it. I didn't know how much time had gone by, but I was starting to sink. *I hope someone is on the other end of the camera so they can come and revive me when I drown.*

I floated, seemingly forever. My arms ached. I was dizzy. I was ready to give up. Then the lights came on and men came through the door. They congratulated me. My time was up. They lowered the ladder, but I was too exhausted to get on it. I put my arms through ladder and they winched me up. I was so exhausted I couldn't walk, and I had to be helped to my feet and to the door. Once in the shower room, all I could do was lie on the floor, trying to gain my feeling back. I learned two things: In the event of a water emergency, pray you can get your life vest on; and, floating with nothing is not only tiring, it's very strenuous on body and mind.

Not all training teaches. Some exercises are only designed to test your mental abilities to cope with different types of stress. I knew I was not claustrophobic, or so I thought. During one exercise, I was taken to an old retired submarine used for training purposes. This doesn't sound so bad, but let me explain some details. First, there were seven of us who went down in this sub. With the exception of the turret, the sub is submerged. We went down to the torpedo hatches. *What the heck is this about?* All the torpedo hatches have big cross handles on them. When opened, the hatch is about six inches of thick steel. The tubes are perfectly round and are not large in diameter by a long shot. Air is pumped into the cylinders, but on the other side of the chute there's water. So if the tube starts to leak, it'll fill with water and you'll drown. This minor detail they mention to you before you're shoved into the tube. If you're nervous about being crammed into a tight place, now you can add drowning to your list of worries.

Again, I was told, "If you wish to quit, now is the time. Once the door is shut, there will be no opening it until your time is up. There is no speaker to cry for help. No communications." Actually, communications are monitored, but you don't know that. You don't know they can hear you, so you assume the worst — if water comes in, you're dead. The instructors could hear everyone crying and screaming for help. I wondered if they just sat back and laughed. I think that's what I'd do.

I was placed head-first into the torpedo tube and the door was closed. I had to stay there for 24 hours. If you have to use the bathroom, you just go in your pants. A lot of us did just that, either out of fear or because we couldn't hold it any longer. I was placed in the tube in my uniform and socks — no boots. My shoulders are wide and it wasn't a good fit. I couldn't even move my hands at my sides. It was very uncomfortable. As soon as the door was shut behind my feet, the eerie feeling started immediately. If you were never claustrophobic, you would be after being placed in this contraption. Inside the smooth cylinder, it was totally dark. I couldn't see the wall two inches in front of me. The sound deprivation was worse. There was only the sound of air coming into the tube — that was it!

I'd been in the chute for only two minutes when I began to feel the effects of claustrophobia. My mind was playing tricks on with me. *What happens if the outside door leaks? Water will start coming in! What happens if they can't open the door or have to try to cut it open? What happens if the air stops coming in? I'll suffocate! What if they forget I'm down here?* All these things and more just kept going through my mind. It started to drive me crazy. I needed something to calm me down. I needed to go to my meditation place — anything to get me out of that thought process.

11

I started by reciting all the Marine Corps cadences that I knew. Once I was done, I sang them again. I tried to sleep, but since I have insomnia, that didn't help. About an hour went by, and of course, I had to pee. I held it for a while, but that didn't last long. I just let it go and filled my torpedo tube with the smell of urine. Thank goodness I didn't have to crap.

The time went by and anxiety crept in. I was starting to wonder when the hell 24 hours would be up. Time just seems to stop when you have no concept of it. *I need something to occupy my time. Okay, I got it – FOOD! What am I going to eat when I get out of this condom?* All that thought did was make me hungry and realize that I wasn't going to eat breakfast, lunch, dinner, midnight snack, midmorning snack… *Ahhhhh, I'm getting hungry.*

The most horrifying sound, or lack thereof, caught me by surprise. The sound of air being fed into the tube was …stopping! *Is the compressor not working right?* I started screaming like a mad man. It was all a ploy. Those bastards wanted to make me think I was going to die. Possibly, I failed that part of the test. I didn't have a good time after that. I kept a keen ear on the air hole. If anything was out of sequence, I was on top of it, yelling at the bastards that I was suffocating. I remember yelling, even though I thought I couldn't be heard, "I need more air! I can't breathe!" I didn't think enough air was being pumped in for me, but there was. I was just freaking myself out. I don't know how long I had been in, but the fart that I'd let out had a lump. The good thing is that we, as people, enjoy our own farts. I sat there for the next hour wondering if I'd shit my pants or the fart was just lingering.

Time was up and the door was opened! Let me tell you, that was one of the greatest moments in my life. The only problem was they were getting others out before me and I wanted out now! Of course, I couldn't move and had to be pulled out. When they finally got to me, I looked around and saw the others standing with shitty, wet pants. The one thing I remember most was the puffy, red eyes of some of the guys. They appeared to have been crying for 24 hours. *At least I'm not that bad. I just peed and shit myself.* All I could think about was food, baby — food!

So, after that exercise I realized that claustrophobia is a great tool in terms of interrogation techniques. I would confidently say that 50% of the participants would have talked. It bothered me, but I could survive. It wasn't the worst that I'd gone through.

Sleep deprivation. What does this term mean? It means going days without sleep and still trying to focus on reality. The Marine Corps has a way to make sure you remember the definition, and that is eight weeks of training. Week one: seven hours of sleep per night; week two: six hours of sleep; week three: five hours. I'm assuming the reader will get the picture and understand that by week eight there is no sleep for one full week.

Sleep deprivation is an effective tool to break an individual down and make them do whatever the interrogator wants. A great interrogation tool for the enemy, but it is also used by the military to brainwash people. You know — give you all the skills that are not accepted in our society anymore, like discipline.

This particular school teaches what you really need to know in the first three to four weeks. After that, it's all a blur. Even today, I couldn't tell you what went on past week four. One funny thing did happen to me. The instructor told me that I was found in the woods and there was this tree stump. If you've ever seen a stump in the woods, it has splits in the top and looks like a sliced pizza. The instructor found me trying to dig out a piece of pizza from the stump.

"Sergeant, what in Hell's name are you attempting to accomplish?" he said.

"Getting a piece of pizza. What does it look like I'm doing?" I replied.

I would love to write more, but I can't remember. I do remember we were kept up doing things all the time, and when it was time to bed down, a guard was posted to stand watch over all of us. Let me rephrase that. The guard wasn't posted to *watch* us, but rather, to teach us a valuable lesson about snoring or talking in your sleep. If you weren't a light sleeper before, you would be after this was over. If you were heard snoring or talking, you were awakened, and made to dress and stand guard for 10 minutes. If you're on your one to two hours' sleep a night phase, 10 minutes is an eternity. After you get no sleep because of snoring or talking, you begin to wake up at the first word or sound you hear. The last thing you want to do is get dressed and stand guard when you're dead on your feet. This might seem like wasted time, but it's a necessity in the field during war. Can you imagine a unit sleeping in a war zone, snoring and talking? Everyone would hear you. One individual could put an entire squad or platoon in danger. After this school, you don't snore, or make *any* sound, for that matter. One peep and you wake yourself up. It's a great tool for the trade of a sniper.

The next training exercise I wouldn't wish on anyone. We were hauled out to the beach at low tide and instructed to start digging foxholes in a specified area. What we weren't told was that the foxholes we were digging were right in line for high tide to wash us out to sea and drown. We were given seven canteens of water, but no food. The only food we'd get was whatever happened to fall into the foxhole. Every training course always had one thing in common: NO FOOD. We were to assume we were taking fire, and our heads were not allowed above the plane of the foxhole — no poking your head up to see what was going on around you. Each individual was by himself in a foxhole, drinking one canteen a day and hoping something resembling food would fall into the hole.

I started digging my hole thinking, ***This is going to be easy***. When I finished, I lay on my back looking at the sun and wondered what all the hype was about. This was a cakewalk! I should've known better. As the tide rose, water started to slowly come over the sides of my foxhole. *What the hell? SHIT! The tide's coming in! Now I get it!* I soon found out what the pain and agony of this week was all about. The tide rises and you spend hours using your helmet to bail out your foxhole or you drown. You don't dare stick your head above the hole plane because then you get docked points and could flunk the school. So I bailed water continuously for hours until I felt my arms would fall off. Of course, there was more. I became extremely wet and was constantly required take off my clothes and socks in an attempt to keep from getting immersion foot (foot rot). As soon as I'd get dry, the water came back to ruin my day. The tide came in and I'd bail. The tide went out and I'd attempt to dry out. This went on for a week. I got very little sleep, was constantly wet, and was starving. Luckily, about every other day some little crab would fall into the hole and I'd have dinner.

Aside from being wet and hungry, even though I ate very little, I still had to use the bathroom. Of course, there was no toilet paper. The best course of action was to leave a small amount of water in my foxhole, relieve myself, and use the sea water to clean my behind. Now it was time to either bail, or sit in a hole with your own excrement floating in it. After one or two times, I got better at it. I figured out to dig one part of the hole a little deeper and keep it full of water. That became my toilet. Everything gets better with education. The other problem that could not be solved was chaffing. I was completely raw from the tiny sand particles. I know it's disgusting, but it's survival. Other than how to set up a toilet in a water-filled foxhole, I learned life in the hole for one week is hell.

My next training was in a more controlled environment — a training pool. The pool is approximately 30' deep. Located next to the pool is a tower with multiple

15

height stages. The top height is probably 40' high. It doesn't look high until you get up there and look down into the water. This setup is to learn evacuation from helos (helicopters) into water. Most helicopters, like the CH-46, have a door in the back that opens. You can parachute out or jump into the water. The helos never get too close to the water's surface because of the rise and fall of the wave swells. Learning the proper way to jump out without hurting yourself is an absolute requirement.

We were started off on the lower level, about 10' off of the water's surface, and given instructions as to the proper way to jump from heights into water.

"Keep your feet together with your toes pointed down to cut through the water. Keep your head straight and put one hand over your mouth and nose to prevent any water entry. It also allows the water to glide by your chin and not knock out a few teeth with impact. Your hand must be properly placed. Hold you palm under your chin with your fingers going up covering your nose."

Now that we all knew how to properly enter the water, the next step was to practice at different heights. Funny thing was, the higher up I got, the harder the water was. It quickly became apparent how very important it was to maintain perfect posture. I watched as one guy jumped from the high tower and landed on his back. They pulled him out. He wasn't seen again. I am sure he was injured, but I never found out how badly. We'd all cringed when he landed improperly, and made a mental note to avoid the same fate, if at all possible.

First level training we started off on the lower tower with our hands tied in the front and our legs tied together. This was great until you hit the water and tried to swim. It takes a little training, but it can be accomplished. The reason for this exercise is in the event you're thrown off a boat as a POW and have to survive in the ocean with your hands and feet tied. This wasn't too bad, but the next training level wasn't fun. For entertainment, we were blindfolded. Before walking to the plank, I was blindfolded and my hands and feet were tied. I stepped out into the black abyss wondering when I'd hit the water. Once I hit, it was time to try and find the top in order to catch my breath. This was all too easy until I was moved to the top tower. It felt like I was falling forever. Unable to see, it was hard to control my hit. A lot of us didn't hit quite right, but the pain was there to let us know we were still alive.

After negotiating jumps from varying heights, we were required to jump with a rifle and pack. This task is actually pretty easy, if done correctly. You must control the jump. I was required to jump from 40' without losing my weapon and pack and attempt to not land on them in order to avoid serious injury. The secret is to jump with the weapon in your right hand and the pack in your left. The pack will float — it's not necessary to strap it onto your back. Strapped to the jumper's back, the extra area of the pack causes you to hit the water like a brick. So, jump, and before you get to the water, release the pack and shove it away from you, tuck the rifle to your side and take the plunge. When you come up, you should be able to find your pack with ease and use it as a floatation device to make your water entry to land.

Once the tower had been mastered, it was time to become familiar with scuba gear. This exercise was quite interesting, to say the least. In the 30'-deep pool, all of your scuba gear is placed at the bottom. Each piece of gear is tagged with a number which is assigned to you. Your responsibility is to swim to the bottom of the pool with 20 other Marines, find all your gear, place it on, and come back to surface.

Once you enter the water and start your descent to the bottom, you are not allowed to come back up without your gear. If you do, you flunk the exercise. We all stared into the pool. The bottom was littered with everyone's gear —

regulators, tanks, masks, fins, weight belts. After diving in, the problem of being down with 20 other men, all attempting to perform the same task, soon became apparent. I found a mask, cleared it, and started looking for my other gear. Someone saw that the mask on my face belonged another man, and he ripped it off my face. That same scenario went for all the other equipment as panic set in. So, the first time we did this, half of the class bailed to the top and almost drowned. It was ugly.

After the third try, we became a team. We helped each other on the bottom, started to share and help find each other's equipment. Water survival, yes — but, unbeknownst to us, at its root, this was a team-building exercise. After the first successful try, it became so easy. Once again, the Marines' emphasis on teamwork was reinforced. There are no individuals. There is only the Corps.

Chapter 2
Scuba Diving, Skydiving & Cultural Exchange
The Fun of Being a Marine

For me, being in the military was fun and adventurous. You either loved it or hated it, and I loved it. Hodge once told me I was like a cat. I had nine lives. I had come close to dying on more than one occasion, and a couple of times I'd had near misses just out having fun.

One incident started down in Mexico, about 60 miles from Camp Pendleton, CA. Marines stationed in Camp Pendleton went to Mexico to let off steam on a regular basis. A group of us went down and ended up drinking all night. We were all drunk, and having the time of our lives. About midnight, when we were returning to base, I decided we should go diving. Unfortunately, I was the only one who thought this was a good idea. Conditions were perfect. It was a slack tide, the ocean looked like a pane of glass, the moon was full, and the temperature was moderate.

I went back to the barracks, grabbed my scuba gear, and headed for Dana Point. Dana Point was a great little cove and the diving there was wonderful. I loaded up my gear and headed out to the water by myself. One rule of thumb in diving is: Never dive alone, because if you have a problem, you have a *serious* problem. I was stubborn and wanted dive. I was an excellent diver, so, avoiding all the rules of safety, I went anyway.

I dove around the rocks looking at the beautiful fish, watching the lobsters, and enjoying the peace and quiet. Well, one thing led to another and I rolled onto my back to watch the full moon. I was down about 30'. Not too deep, but more than deep enough if you have trouble. I was rocking back and forth gently with the surge of the ocean, looking up at the moon, and since I was still drunk, I passed out.

The next thing I remember was not being able to breathe. I woke up choking, gagging, and wondering where I was. I had forgotten I was diving. I looked around and quickly realized I was underwater. I didn't have a clue what depth I was at. I dumped my weight belt and bolted to the top for air. I finally reached the surface, and to my surprise, I was alone. I had completely forgotten that I'd gone diving *alone*. I swam back to the beach and lay down, gasping for air and wondering what the hell I was doing diving drunk and alone. This was a wakeup call, but only not to dive drunk and alone. I would like to say I never again dove drunk, but that was still an every weekend thrill. I did, however, dive with a buddy from then on. It's always better to dive drunk with a friend. When I look back at that incident, I wonder how I didn't end up dead. As a whole, a lot of us felt we were indestructible, and I was probably the worst.

Later in my career, I was stationed in Japan with the 3rd Recon Battalion at Camp Hansen. There is a beautiful spot there called Kin Blue Beach. One year prior to my being stationed there, the second largest great white shark ever recorded had been caught at Kin Blue. We always dove there. It was a thrill wondering if we were going to see the next big great white, but the lobsters were the main attraction. You could catch lobsters the size of your leg.

Kin Blue was exceptionally clear and had a reef just two yards out. The reef was from 15' to 70' deep. There was a small cliff that overlooked the reef and you could see right down into the water. The cliff was handy. If you got separated from your buddy, all you had to do was get out of the water, climb to the top and look around. Normally, with the dive lights, you could spot another diver quite well.

One beautiful night we had a nice moon and slack

tide. My friend and I decided it was time to go out and find some lobsters for a weekend BBQ. We made it a point, if we got separated, to come up after about five to 10 minutes. Normally one would come up after about one minute of separation, but if we'd done that, we would constantly be returning to the surface. Being experienced divers, my partner and I often separated.

We went into the water with our big dive lights, spear guns, and a giant dive bag for all the lobster. The lobsters were plentiful that night, and of course, as usual, my partner and I separated. I was diving in search of lobsters when, out of the blue, I saw the largest octopus I'd ever seen. I estimated he was probably about five feet long from tip to head. I knew that our Mama San, the Japanese lady that kept our barracks, would love to have him. It was my duty to capture this octopus and bring it home to her for her family.

The octopus was slinking along trying to get away from my dive light. I pulled out my spear gun and took aim. When trying to hit an octopus, its big bubble is just an air sack. In order to kill it, you need to hit the part of the body that is in the middle connected to the legs. That's where the brain center is. Unaware of this at the time, I took careful aim and hit it in the air sack.

The octopus was pissed off, and rightfully so. He stood up on all tentacles and turned a ghostly white. I knew he was pissed, so I tried to recover my spear by reeling in my line, which only brought the now irate octopus closer to me. The fight was on. He wrapped his tentacles around me and tried to bite me with his little mouth. My dive light was strapped to my wrist. Had I let go, the light would float around and shine everywhere. In the meantime, my partner had run out of air and was up top looking for me. It must have been a hell of a sight from up top. Imagine looking down and seeing your buddy's light going all over the place. My partner's first thought? Shark! So, he called the shore patrol.

I was still on the bottom fighting with the octopus. His tentacles were stuck all over me, trying to rip off my regulator and mask. I reached down, grabbed my knife, and started to cut. I cut my wet suit and myself in an attempt to try and kill the crazy octopus. He managed to pull my regulator out of my mouth, nearly causing me to drown. Luckily, I had time to grab my spare. I finally killed the octopus and it was time for me to try and make it back to land. I slowly made it back to the beach where there were three cars with flashing lights and people suiting up to come and get me. I walked up with tentacles hanging off of me and the entire crowd staring. I had cut up my suit, the octopus was cut up. It was a mess. Everyone came running over and started asking, all of them at once, what the hell happened. I took the time to let everyone know not to shoot octopuses in the air sack — it makes them extremely pissed off.

The entire incident was the laugh of the barracks for months to come. We finally named the mean-ass octopus Brutus. Lesson: If you don't have the right tools, let it go. I damn near died.

Marines that dive live by the ocean and dive all the time. The ocean is wonderful and exciting. My buddy and I decided to go diving at Diver's Cove outside of Camp Pendleton. We intended to make a night dive at high tide. Our location of choice was a reef situated about a mile out, which, when you're young and in shape, is not that far of a swim. The reef was about a 60' dive and was teeming with lobster and abalone.

When making a dive, one should always have a compass. Mine happened to be broken, and I didn't consider really needing one. We had made dives on this site so many times it was like being in our own backyard. Besides, surely my diving partner, John, would have one.

We swam out and down we went. We separated and started looking for lobster. After about an hour, it was time to come up, locate my buddy, and get back to land. Normally you would want to start your ascent with 500lbs. I made it up to the top with less than 100lbs. There was no going back down — I was completely out of air.

When I reached the surface, the fog had moved in. I couldn't see five feet in front of me. I started to yell for John and could hear him yelling back, but it was hard to tell how far or in which direction he was. When you're on top of the water, the current will drag you out to sea or push you into land — one or the other. John must have been up top for a while, because he was about 200-300 yards away from me.

We continued yelling to each other, trying to swim toward each other. After about 20 minutes, we reunited. We clamped onto one another and started to try to figure which way to shore. John immediately suggested that I use my compass and swim us in. I reminded him that mine was broken. He informed me he didn't have one. This was a fine predicament. No compass and neither one of us knew which way it was to land!

The fog was so thick we couldn't make out lights on shore, or anything else for that matter. We were probably floating farther and farther out to sea, so we decided to drop our little buoy in the water and see which way the current took it. The buoy was much lighter and would be carried fast by the current, so at least we could get some idea of the current and land. If we had seen this coming, we could have easily made our way to land underwater. It's easy to tell the direction of land by the riffles in the sand. Since we couldn't see bottom, we had to trust the current method. I dropped the buoy in and we watched it cruise by us. We set out in the opposite direction and prayed it was toward land.

We swam for about 1 1/2 hours, periodically dropping the buoy to make sure we were heading in the right direction. Then we saw the most beautiful sight — lights! We swam for another hour and finally made it to shore. As we approached shore, we realized we had been floating down current for a while. We didn't recognize where we had come ashore. We looked around and figured one of us had to stay with the gear and the other could go back for the car — we were way too far away to pack all that gear. We carried the gear up to the road and John stripped off to his shorts. I stayed with the gear and John took off.

After a couple of hours John returned.

"What took you so long?"

"I got here pretty quick. We floated about five miles down the coast."

The lesson? Always dive with a compass AND a backup. We were lucky that we weren't carried out to sea. We were out too far and had no navigation. Bad move on our part. Needless to say, we both went and got new compasses.

Skydiving was a standard in the Marine Corps. Normally, when skydiving in the military, you dive with main chute and a reserve chute. We used a chute called a "1½ Bravo." The chute was made with a main canopy and a reserve. If you got into trouble with your main canopy, you rotated a knob located on the rigging 1.5 turns, punched out the main canopy, and pulled your reserve.

Once again, I was down in Mexico drinking with the boys and didn't make it back until the wee hours of the morning. Notice how most of the "life risking" starts out this way? We got home, all of us still drunk. The Staff Sergeant came in shouting that we had a morning jump. I was drunk, and had had no sleep, so I filled my canteens with vodka and orange juice and left for the hanger. We went to the chute hanger and packed our chutes. By now, I had probably made over 100 jumps, so I was pretty salty. I crammed a chute into a parachute pack, not making much of an effort to do it correctly. I figured I had a spare. Little did I know I was going to need it.

We loaded up in a C-130 and off we went. I think we were at about 12,000 feet. No need for oxygen, just a straight morning dive and then we could go back, clean our gear, and I could go to bed. We performed our HALO jump (High Altitude Low Opening). Watching my altimeter gauge, when I reached about 1,200 feet, I pulled the chute and stayed in my tuck. *Whooooooffff.* I looked up and saw my toggles and lines were tangled. SHIT! I punched out my main canopy and ripped my spare. The spare is much smaller, meaning I needed plenty of time and altitude to grab the canopy and slow my butt down. In this case, I pulled way too late and the canopy didn't have much time to do its job. I knew I was going to hit hard. I woke up a little later hanging in a tree with my buddies screaming at me. It seems that my spare canopy caught some trees, which saved my life. Unfortunately, it also swung me into the tree, knocking me out. In my leg pouch I carried a rope for just such an emergency. The rope is to repel out, should you happen to get stuck in a tree. I had never had to do this, but I was too high to just drop to the ground.

I hooked my rope onto the chute, put on my carabineer, released myself from the tree, and repelled down. It wasn't a pretty sight when I got down. I could have been in big trouble, but my Staff Sergeant believed in keeping things at a low level. I cleaned dishes for the next few weeks. One thing about having a tight organization; we take care of our own. What happens in the field stays in the field.

I'd like to tell a story about my experience with a Japanese Sensei. I had studied martial arts back in the states, Kung Fu, in particular. The Marines taught me tons of self-defense, so I considered myself a trained killer. I was the toughest thing alive. Little did I know I was wrong in my assumptions. I think one might have called me arrogant and stupid.

I was deployed to 3rd Recon Battalion in Okinawa, Japan. Our ranking Colonel was a Japanese-American. Aware that I was into martial arts, he asked me if I would like the opportunity to train in a Japanese Dojo. What

American wouldn't? I didn't realize that an arrogant, cocky Marine like me needed this to get my attitude into proper prospective — but the Colonel knew it and thought the experience would be a valuable lesson for me.

The Dojo was located outside of Camp Hansen. The Sensei was Master Lou. He spoke little English and I didn't speak Japanese, so communication was a problem. I approached the Dojo, walked in, and did my respectful bow. I noticed several of the Japanese students staring at me. I am sure they wondered why I was in their place of worship. The energy and discipline in this place was the greatest that I have ever experienced. I don't know how to explain the feeling, but it was intense.

The old man made his way over to me, bowed, and began to speak to me in broken English. I told him my Colonel instructed me to come and train there for a while. He said, "Oh yes, he said that you would be coming. Have you studied any martial arts before?"

"I have a Black Belt."

He asked me to demonstrate.

I thought he meant American sparring. WRONG. In Japan, there are only two belts, White and Black. A student may be a white belt, but has yet to receive his black belt. In the U.S., students receive different colored belts as a show of rank — and so the student will have to pay for each in order to advance. The Japanese view martial arts as a way of life, not a scheme to make money.

Master Lou clapped his hands and three white belts came out. Each of the three was half my size. This was going to be way too easy. I got ready to point spar, but these guys didn't play. They beat the crap out of me, damn near broke my nose, and almost caved in my ribs. *What the hell is this about?* Master Lou clapped, I got up slowly, made my way to the door, and left.

The next day I ran into the Colonel. He asked me how the lesson went.

"I'm not going back. They basically beat the crap out of me and humiliated me."

"I had to beg Master Lou to allow you train with them. You are not about to humiliate me by showing disrespect and not going back."

What was I to do? This was an order. That night, I made my way back to the Dojo. Again Master Lou met me and asked had I ever studied Martial Arts. I responded, "Yes, I have a black belt." He again asked me to demonstrate. Now that I knew the game, it was not a problem. I'd demonstrate and beat the hell out of those little bastards.

He clapped, the three students stepped out and commenced to turning me inside out, kicking and hitting me in places that I didn't even know I had. I never knew you could hurt in so many areas. He clapped again and I was released to hide my shame and crawl out the door.

I knew I couldn't go ask the Colonel to release me. The next day I went back to the Dojo with hurting ribs, a cracked nose, and a black and blue wrist. I entered the Dojo and there they all were, disciplined and training with precision. Master Lou made his way over to me and bowed. He made a few comments. "It is good to see you are back. This means you have some discipline. This is the beginning of a good martial artist. Now, you know some martial arts?"

I stopped him in mid sentence and said, "Sir, I do not know any martial arts."

Master Lou looked at me and smiled. "Now you have learned! Your tea pot was too full. It could not take on any more knowledge. Now that you are empty, you can learn and fill your pot with good knowledge."

I felt like an idiot. All this time I thought they just hated me. But the shame I felt was nothing like what would come in the next few months of training.

For the next five months I trained in the Dojo. Not under Master Lou, but under some of his more experienced black belts. Master Lou, of course, supervised. During this time, it was Naugi, the one being trained, and Ooki, the one training. In that respect, I was always the Naugi, getting beaten on by everyone in the Dojo. I figured this was because I was a big white guy, a Marine, and they wanted to practice their techniques on me, just to make sure they worked. Well, they did and they used pressure points for everything. Not only were my wrists sore, but my arms and legs were black and blue.

This went on for five months. I never got to train, but was always subjected to pain. I didn't understand the reasoning, so I opened my big mouth and questioned the Sensei of the Dojo. I went over one night after class and asked Master Lou why I never got to train. Why was I always the one being thrown around? This didn't go over very well.

"Americans always have to question everything that they know nothing about. They cannot rely on the one teaching. Perhaps he knows what he is doing. Americans are arrogant and have no discipline."

"I don't understand."

"You are being trained. You must catch up to the other students."

"I don't learn any of the moves."

"You must have the moves done to you a thousand times. You must know that they are true. You must know that they work. You must know how to apply them properly. Do you know where large intestinal #4 is located?"

This is a pressure point, so I pointed right to it.

"Does it hurt?"

I said it did.

"What does it heal?"

I said headaches.

"Do you still know nothing?"

I respectfully bowed, hung my head in shame, and never again asked a question. I learned a valuable lesson: It is more important to listen than to ask.

Socrates said it best: "I am the smartest man in the world because I know nothing." He was right. Just when you think you know something, you find you really don't know anything. I learned my lesson about discipline and respect from the Japanese. They are one of the greatest cultures that I have ever seen.

Some of my fondest memories were of the South Koreans. I was deployed to the Korean DMZ because the military decided that the South Koreans needed Marines living with them. We would live and eat with them and the government subsidized the family for us staying there. Every morning a bus would pick us up. We would take care of our duties on base, then be dropped off to live with our Korean families. We helped them work during the evening and on the weekends. This little adventure lasted about six weeks.

I didn't get a family with a pretty daughter. My family was an old couple in their 70s. The house had a dirt floor. A fire pit was dug down about two feet and had vents under the floor. This was how floors were heated in Korea. It would get down to 20 below, so a heated floor was a nice feature. The yard was about the size of a normal bathroom and held the family's milk cow. The cow didn't get to move around much.

The first night and the first meal with the Koreans will be ingrained in my memory for the rest of my life. They were cooking something in the pot. Whatever it was, it stunk. There were three bowls, two little ones and one big one. I began to wish they would just let me starve at night — it would have been better than eating their cooking. I sat there waiting for the smelly stuff to hit the table. Rice was served first, accompanied by unrecognizable fish. Not a gutted fish, a fish head. They simply cut off the head and placed it on my rice. Talk about fish heads and rice, well ... there it was.

I looked down at the bowl wondering if I had what it took to eat this without throwing up. I started by eating the rice and picking at the fish. I finished the rice, but barely touched the fish. The old man looked at his wife and then said something to me. He took my bowl and started picking my fish head with his fingers. He pulled out the eyes, dug out the meat, and then placed it back in the bowl. The fish head was quickly boned out. He reached over, gave me more rice and handed back the bowl. *FUCK ME!* I choked it down, but they looked genuinely pleased that I'd eaten their disgusting food.

This went on for the week. I don't want to bore you about all the gross food they ate, some of which I am sure was dog. I just tried to block it out.

My next experience was truly amazing. These old Koreans had a cart which they used to carry wood and grain. I thought they got supplies from the market, but I was wrong. One day the old man got the cart, and with the old women and me following, off we went. We had been hiking for a while when we came upon a big mountain — or should I say, a *steep* mountain. Being a fit and tough Marine, I offered to drag the cart up the hill. We started up the hill, and about halfway up I was running out of juice and started to slow down. The old man came over, motioned me off, took hold of the cart and cruised up the hill. How embarrassing! As if that weren't bad enough, then the old woman took the cart! *What the hell are these people made of?* For the entire day, we gathered wood and grain along the roadside, or at least what could be found.

The next morning I was sore and still thinking of the mountain I had climbed. We got up at the usual time, 5:00 AM. We went out and loaded up the cart again. This time, I was ready. Where do we go? Right back to that same mountain! What was it with these people? I decided I needed to buy them some rice and food. To hell with this mountain! I took the cart and drug it about halfway up, then the old woman took over. I felt like shooting myself. We gathered up all our supplies, and headed back down the mountain again.

That night, I was overjoyed that I was going back to the base. Damn the mountain. Over the next five weeks, I became accustomed to the mountain. I could have made it after about the 3rd week, but the man and woman wouldn't let me. I guess that's how they kept in such good shape. It floors me how easy we have it the states. These people knew suffering and hard work, something we Americans forgot with the arrival of Burger King and Welfare. I grew up at a rapid pace. I started to see the world for what it was. I become more thankful for what I had and more sympathetic for those who didn't have it as good. I have great respect for the Koreans. They are a very hard-working and kind people.

Chapter 3
Hazing & Tradition

During the years I spent in the Corps, hazing and Marine traditions were a great part of team building. Some of the liberal pukes might call it horrible and inhumane. Remember, liberals aren't in the military. They're usually found in Canada if a war happens to break out. I'll tell you some of the hazing that goes on, and let you decide.

I remember the first time I was subjected to hazing and tradition. I was in Fort Bennington, VA, and I had just earned my jump wings. It has been a Marine tradition, since the inception of jump school, for the men in your platoon that have their wings to beat the wings into your chest. Upon returning as a graduate from jump school, all the men in your platoon welcome you back and the ceremony begins. This is something you beg for, not run away from. I was so excited for my friends and superiors to pound my wings into my chest, I couldn't wait. An outsider might ask why, but unless you've experienced it, it's hard to understand. The ceremony is a way of being accepted by your peers and superiors; something akin to an initiation into a special fraternity. The other members have gone through the same thing. Once you've been initiated, you become a full-fledged member and have the right to participate in the next initiation.

The gauntlet is set up; 20 Marines standing in a line. The jump wings are sticking in your uniform just above your left breast pocket. There are no backings on the wings, so the pins will stick into your chest. It begins. Each man walks up, congratulates you, welcomes you to the jump squad and then hits you as hard as they can on the wings. You stand there and take it, proving you're a Marine and proud of it. I loved it.

When the ceremony was finished, I took off my shirt and found that my chest was black and blue. Blood covered my shirt and chest. Hazing? No. This is tradition and I loved every minute of it. This is a way to make Marines feel pain, deal with pain, and know that many others have gone through the same thing before them. It's an admission that what was good enough for the Marines before me is good enough for me.

Sometime after I received my wings, I heard either a Marine or an Army regular complained about the pinning ceremony, and the tradition had to officially stop. While it might have stopped in the public eye, it was still in full force behind close doors. It was a shame this wimp of a man ruined such a great tradition. In my opinion, this makes our military weaker. Pukes like that should be beaten and thrown out of the country. They make me sick. This was tradition. It built camaraderie, we all loved it, and it was such a great pleasure to be part of. I feel sorry for those who cannot be part of a military that once upheld traditions and love of country.

Another great Marine tradition was receiving the blood stripe. This takes place when a Marine receives their NCO status (Non-commissioned Officer). In a previous war, most of the Marine Corps' NCOs were killed. To honor and remember those NCOs, the Marines place a red stripe down the legs of their dress uniforms. The next time you see a Marine in dress blues, look at the legs. You will see a red stripe going down the outside of each leg. It is a symbol that Marines don't forget their fallen.

In the Marine Corps, the rank of Lance Corporal, an E-3, is not an NCO. Upon attaining the rank of Corporal, a Marine becomes an NCO and has earned the right to wear the blood stripe on their uniform. All Marines want this. They want their stripes. The new NCO has earned the right to the blood stripe ceremony.

How do you earn the blood stripe? A gauntlet,

composed of all the other NCOs, is set up. The new NCO steps into the gauntlet with an NCO on each side. The NCOs count and knee the new NCO as hard as they can in the legs. Continuing to walk down the gauntlet, this is repeated by as many NCOs as there are in the line. At the end of the line, the new NCO turns, and if he has the guts, walks back through the gauntlet. I walked up and back. I couldn't walk for a few days, but I was very proud of my blood stripes. I showed everyone. God bless tradition and to hell with the liberals.

The Marines actually did haze. Generally, this was done every time a new private came into the platoon. His first time in the field, he was greatly hazed. This was the welcome to our platoon initiation. How well he took it depended on how well or how long the hazing lasted. The ones who took it like a man weren't punished like the ones who cried about it.

The general public doesn't understand that war is hard. There isn't some liberal in Washington fighting next to you, or some goof from the local draft board. These men were brave enough to enlist. It was our job to make them fighting men and not allow them to remain wimps. The Marines needed men that would save our lives and be willing to give up their lives for each other. This is something that the general populace can't understand. Politicians certainly don't understand it. To most, we were numbers — just a large corporation. In the business world, it's easy to fire someone you don't know, but to the individual fired, the act is devastating. A government sending men to war is easy because no one making the decision is doing the fighting or the dying. It's just a number. I only wish the government and most Americans loved me and the Marines as much as we love them.

Chapter 4
Preparing for War

Life in the Marines was full of adventure, some scary and some just plain fun. For the most part, everything a Marine goes through serves one purpose — to prepare for war. You are made physically able, and most of all, mentally ready. The Marines that I knew were kids off the street. They were brought in and made into men. The Corps gave them all the brainwashing and training I have written about earlier. It's funny, when you're out driving all you see is USMC stickers on vehicles. Marines are proud. Marines are forever. There are no ex-Marines.

As I look back at the training to prepare for battle, the building of camaraderie, teamwork, physical fitness, and building of mental attitude, I would say the most important aspect that a Marine needs is the mental fortitude to finish a mission.

Is there anything you can do to prepare yourself for actual combat? I wish I could say there was, but we all know different. Training and preparation are necessary, but until you're actually in combat, nothing will prepare a soldier for what he may face. I remember, prior to deployment for Desert Storm, an old Vietnam vet telling us, "No one really knows how they're going to act in actual combat. All you can hope for is that you'll act as you were trained." From personal experience, I can say that most people don't initially act the way they were trained, but they come around later. You have no choice — you either come around...or die.

So, how do you train for war? I've written about schools and training, but there's more to it than that. Not all Marines go to the specialty schools, and they need training, as well. Obstacle training is an every-week practice in the

Marines. An obstacle course consists of repelling towers, rope swings, running on poles, diving on nets, climbing a tower, and hand-over-hand down a rope. Each of these has a particular reason for its design. The reason for repelling is a given. All Marines must know how to repel in case we come to a cliff and need to get down, or if we're required to make a window entry and have to repel down a building. The rope swing helps prepare for crossing chasms. In the jungle there are vines that are extremely strong. They are excellent for crossing streams or cliffs. Running on poles prepares you for moving in the woods or jungle. This is an obstacle that will be present all the time, and it improves balance and mental ability to perform in the woods.

War games were another form of preparation. With our weapons loaded down with blanks, we would play war with other units. One particular war game we played on the side of Interstate Highway 5. My whole platoon and I were out in the field for approximately 14 days fighting battles with another company. One night Hodge and I were out on patrol looking for activity. I had an M-60 machine gun and Hodge had a SAW (squad automatic weapon), both loaded down with blanks.

We were scouting the area next to I-5 when we heard talking. We crept up, got within hearing distance, and discovered a group of illegal aliens. The border patrol station was about a mile from our location, so we decided to have some fun and bring them in. We jumped up with those automatic weapons and let the fire ring. Flames were shooting out of our guns and the illegals hit the deck screaming. We made them hold their hands up and marched them to the border patrol station, all the time with weapons full of blanks. When we went back, they had left all their belongings on the ground. We pillage through them and found a nice big bottle of perfume. Hodge and I sprayed that whole thing on each other. We smelled like French hookers that hadn't showered for a month. As Hodge and I made our way back into camp, one of the guys woke up and said, "Damn! You smell that chick that just drove by?" Of course, we laughed. It didn't end there. For the next couple of days, the guys kept telling us how good we smelled.

War games were good. They made you think. There are tricks of the trade you learn, as well. For example, when attacking at night we, or the enemy, will shoot up daylight clusters in order to see. If you look straight into them, your night vision is gone. It'll take twenty minutes to regain it. The trick is to keep one eye closed while the cluster is burning, and keep the other eye open so you don't get run over. To illustrate how this technique works, get up at night and try this experiment. Walk over to the fridge, close one eye, open the door and then quickly close it. You'll retain night vision in your closed eye, but not in the open eye. If you try to walk back to bed with the eye you kept open, you can't see. All you have to do is open the eye that you had closed and you'll see fine. Great trick.

Another neat trick was given to me by an old Gunnery Sergeant. Ever have the feeling you were being watched? If so, it's because someone's staring at your head. I guess you might say brain waves are flowing back and forth. If you intend to sneak up on an individual from behind, stare at their back or butt. They will never turn around. As soon as you stare at their head, they'll have the feeling of being watched and will turn around every time. I know this works because I've tried it many times.

One of the most important skills that all Marines must learn is to navigate with a compass. This is one skill that is taught over and over. I'm not going try to teach a course on how to use a compass, but I will briefly explain some of its uses, besides telling you where North is located.

First, there's resection. Assume you don't know your exact location on a map, but you do see two hills you recognize on the map. Hold your compass out and shoot an angle at one mountaintop, look at the other mountaintop, and you get two angles. So, for example, looking at mountain A you find you are located at 187° and facing mountain B, you are located at 259°. Now comes the easy part. Take a protractor, find mountain A and draw a line backwards at 187° angle. Do the same for mountain B, and where the lines cross is your location.

Now if resection wasn't confusing enough, let's talk about intersection. Say you see the enemy "X" miles away and want to bomb their location. In order to successfully locate fire, you need the grid to their location. This process is the reverse of a resection. You get onto two known points and shoot azimuths from each point to the enemy's location. For example: You know the location of a mountain on which you're sitting. Look at the enemy and shoot an angle, say 122°. Now you need to move to another known location, preferably another mountaintop, and shoot another angle, let's say 210°. Using a protractor, plot the lines from the two locations on the map, and where they intersect is the enemy's location. Now you're ready to call in for an air strike, or to just report the enemy's precise location.

A great game we'd play is called KIIM (Keep It In Memory). This is a tool of nearly unequaled value. It's hard at the beginning, but after a few tries, you can become very proficient at it. This is how it works. Members in your squad walk down a trail, putting things like ammo cans, socks, uniforms, food, knives and so forth into position along the trail. Your mission is to walk down the trail without stopping, and try to observe as much as possible. To start, you walk down the path for approximately one mile. You're not allowed to write anything down — that takes too much time. Keep it in your memory (KIIM). At the end of the trail, you're required to write down what you observed. You'll be shocked at all the things you missed. This part of KIIM is easy. It gets worse. Next, different objects are placed along the path. You walk the trail, same as before, but when you get to the end you're required to run, do pushups, do sit ups, go for a swim, or dig a foxhole. The longer the game goes on the worse it gets. At the start of KIIM, you're only using your short-term memory — now you're trying to develop your long-term memory. Believe it or not, you will forget half of what you observed. In order to gain this skill, you must practice every day, no matter where you are. For example, if you walk into a store, look at everyone there, sit at a table and try and remember what everyone is doing. It takes a long time to attain this skill, and it takes a very long time to really master it. Once mastered, it is one of the best skills you can have in combat. Nothing will get by you. Just one small article out of place can give the enemy away.

Chapter 5
The Savior

10 May, 1988 – 1000 Hours
I was one of a select few special operations snipers for the USMC. I was only 21 at the time when I was called to special meeting with high-ranking officials. All persons selected to attend were called in individually.

"Corporal?" the board asked.

"Yes," I replied.

"Please have a seat."

I took a seat in the chair wondering how many others had sat in the same chair just hours before me.

"Corporal, you understand that the country needs your assistance?"

I recalled thinking, *What could this great nation need from a peon like me?*

They spoke to me as an equal, asking several unrelated questions to get me to relax. Then the room went from warm to cold.

"Corporal, everything said in this room from here on out is strictly confidential."

"Yes, sir." I took my own vow of confidentiality, swearing not to discuss any part of the meeting with my colleagues or anyone else.

They proceeded with the inquiry.

"Corporal, as you may know, drugs are becoming a major issue not only in our country, but in many other parts of the world. The time is at hand for America to take action on those who wish to do us harm. Do you agree?"

"Yes."

"It is with great concern that our country tries to eliminate and slow the problem. These people have no regard for the civilized world. They subject our families and friends to the ugliness that possesses our society."

At that moment I realized what was happening. They where gauging my response to their assertion that our society was in danger of collapsing through the trafficking and abuse of illegal narcotics. I had to agree or they would probably stop the inquiry and dismiss me. They were testing me. I passed with flying colors.

"Corporal, we have an glorious opportunity before us. Not only can we help our country, but our neighbors, as well. The time has come to send in a special operations unit to bring down some of the drug trafficking. This, Corporal, is where we ask for your participation and help."

"I am ready for whatever you ask me to do." I knew my job. I had only one job, and that was to kill.

"The fact is, Corporal, that a select few have been given a great opportunity to provide personal security for this country and take whatever means necessary to enforce our laws. Your mission is to sit on the border of Honduras and El Salvador. Supply whatever resistance is required to those who travel over the border."

"Sir, is 'resistance' considered lethal force?"

"That is correct."

My first thought was of James Bond; a license to kill and none of society's consequences.

"Corporal, do you have a problem with this?"

"None, sir." As I looked up, I simply asked, "How will I know?"

"You'll know. We are not going to leave you in the dark out there. You will have Intel. There will be instructors coming in to give you some special classes on recognition of potential drug and gunrunners. They will offer habits, typical vehicles used, and where they will be traveling. In the next few weeks you will be well-versed in what to look for and how to recognize these select individuals."

The interview continued with questions about my religion and family. My answers were crafted with the

41

information I thought they wanted to hear. I couldn't comprehend the governmental latitude and authority I was given for this mission. This was like being the main character in a movie. I was now James Bond, secret agent, out to save the world. I did not comprehend the haunting quality of the events that would follow. My conscience would be forever plagued by the consequences of my actions.

I recall hunting deer and elk all my life. These were some of my earliest memories. This was different. This was the ultimate hunt. For the first time, more than any dangerous game, my quarry processed the same ability to reason and think as I. It was the ultimate challenge. The adrenaline rushed through my veins, and at times I felt as though it had replaced my blood. I had to keep this in check. This was for my country and family, wasn't it? This was my justification. As I prepared, I convinced myself that what I was about to do was my patriotic duty. What do you say when the career you have chosen and have been trained to do is to kill another human being? Later, I would reflect and consider the possibility that this mission was for some political or monetary gain.

We loaded a C-130 prior to sundown. A quick taxi out and we were off. Inside with me were nine Marines, all of us going to the same place — Hell. We had completed our training and had been given orders on where to go and how far we could travel. Each of us had a mission, a partner, and a route to follow. Hodge, my partner, and I had been assigned approximately 60 miles of connecting roads on the border side of Honduras and El Salvador. Each team's mission had the same specific goal: Stay in our designated area for approximately one month and control the borders at all cost. What the hell was that supposed to mean? Kill everyone who might pose a potential problem? The orders further stated, "There will be a specific drop point for food, water, orders and ammunition. Each drop will be made on a predetermined day to be communicated to you at a later date. Have a good and safe mission. Leave no sign of American Marines in the area. Semper Fi."

There were two lights in the transport plane; one red, one green. Red means stand by. Green means go. The green light came on, telling Hodge and me it was time to jump. I looked out into the dark opening thinking it was the opening of the bowels of Hell. My assessment wasn't far from wrong. We leapt into the darkness, unaware of what was to follow. As the darkness folded around me and my eyes came into focus, I became aware of an eerie god-like feeling. Were we to be the avenging angles sent to deal our wrath on the perpetrators of evil? Free-falling, like birds without wings, the ground slowly came into view. A quick glance at my altimeter showed 1,000 feet. Time to pull the chute. I pulled my ripcord and the canopy came alive, opening like a leaf in the wind. Hodge flew past me, a combination of his forward speed and my sudden deceleration. I saw Hodge's chute open immediately below me. As my descent slowed, the wind became warm and peace settled in with the soaring of my glide. We touched down and secured our chutes for later retrieval. The adventure was about to start.

"Hodge, you okay?"

"Yeah, just a little nervous I guess."

"Me too, Hodge, me too."

We sat down in the total darkness, gathered our belongings, and did an inventory of our weapons, tools, and equipment.

"Hodge, let's not travel at night yet. Let's try to get some sleep and in the morning we can find out our exact location and go from there."

He agreed without any argument. Hodge and I were both 21, but he was not as gung-ho as I. He was more conservative, smaller in stature, and generally more compassionate in nature. I was more mean and aggressive toward everything. I had the drive to go out and accomplish

43

the mission with no regrets. Hodge would obey his orders and accomplish his mission, but he didn't necessarily take pleasure in the job.

Hodge grew up in the all-American family. He had two older brothers and one younger sister. They were a very religious family with a well-structured home life. He told me many times why he joined the Corps. During his confessions, he always called me "Finger," the nickname I received during weapons training. I was so dubbed because of my habit of holding my trigger finger up every time I scored a bull's-eye. I would joke with the guys in class that my finger was worth millions to the government and I wasn't allowed to put it in my pocket because it was a concealed weapon. So, needless to say, "Finger" stuck with me.

"Finger, the only reason I did this is because of my family."

"Why would you say that?"

"My family always talked about Grandpa. They admired him so much. He was a hero in the Great War, and a tough-as-they-came Marine. My brothers never went into the military, but they were good athletes and what everyone considered a boy to be. I wasn't. They picked on me — called me Hodgy the little Ethiopian boy. I guess I wanted to show them all, so I joined the Marines. My father once told me, 'Son you're not your brothers or your Grandpa. Maybe try the National Guard first.' After that I was so frustrated by family's lack of confidence that nothing could stop me. I told them I was joining the Marines and I wanted to be in recon. All the drive and hard work it took to get me here, and my family still doesn't believe it."

"Hodge, I can't sleep."

"Me either."

"Hodge, can you believe we're here? What we're asked to do?"

"I tell you what Finger, if and when we get out of here, I am going home."

"Going home for what, Hodge?"

"This has brought light into my life. It isn't for me."

"Hodge, are you going to be able to complete this mission?"

"I don't know."

"Why the hell did you come?"

"Finger, you just wouldn't understand."

"Try me!"

"Okay, I just wanted to know if I could do this. Could I be a man and do what is required? Kill another human being?"

"Hodge, I feel the same way, too. We won't know until the time comes. I'm sure that when the time comes you will know what to do, and will do it."

"Bob, these people don't even know we are here. They're like a herd of cattle. It's not like they are going to be shooting back or anything. This isn't even war."

"Whoa, listen Hodge, it is war! They affect U.S. citizens' everyday lives! Kids die every day due to drugs and garbage they send into our country! We have a chance to save some of the lives they destroy!"

"Bob, do you really believe that crap? As soon as one dies, there'll be 10 to take his place!"

"I know, Hodge, but we can let them know we are trying to stop it. Make it harder for them."

"Yeah, I guess you're right. Let's go to sleep, Bob. I'm tired."

The next day came all too quickly. We gathered up all the goodies and started off using our GPS. Intel had provided a few locations, and I suggested a mountaintop approximately 700 yards from an intersection. By the look of the map, the mountaintop had a great view from all directions, and plenty of cover for protection. Plus, we had the advantage of the high ground.

Our equipment consisted of gillie suits made from burlap and leather for camouflage purposes, a camera with telescopic lenses to take recon photos and to confirm kills, a spotting scope, Marine Corps knives (K-Bar), a radio, GPS, food, water, weapons, and ammunition.

We started off up a long canyon that was covered with dense tropical foliage. The jungle was alive with all kinds of bugs and creatures. A person who was claustrophobic would freak out in this place. The humidity was awful, and the mosquitoes constantly harassed us, hoping to get a nice meal. I led the way as we crawled our way up the canyon, and Hodge trailed behind.

"Hodge, what's going on?"

"Finger, this ain't right."

"What the hell are you going to do then?"

"I don't know."

"Look Hodge, come with me. You won't have to do anything you don't want to."

Well, after that Hodge kept right up with me and told me thanks for understanding. My only thought was how he got by the board with this attitude. I was getting aggravated, and worried that Hodge's reluctance would land us both in a tight spot.

We finally made it to the top, and by the looks of the GPS, we had about eight miles to go.

"Bob, let's stay off the high ground. Stay lower and walk around the mountain."

Made good sense to me. I didn't want to have my silhouette sticking out there for everyone to see.

"What do you think the other reconnaissance teams are doing right now?" I said.

"Shooting like open season, Bob."

"I have to tell you, it doesn't make it any easier to do my job with you moping around."

"Well, I just don't think we are doing the right thing."

"You have to look at it as these people are trying to kill you and your family."

"I know, Bob, I know. I'm just having a hard time with it right now. Guess I never really thought I would have to do this for real."

"Well, you chose your profession. Same as I did. Now let's do it, jarhead, or go home and face the consequences!"

Finally, after another day of hiking, we made it to within one mile of our objective.

"Hodge, let's stop here and bed down for the night."

"Sounds good to me."

"Well, my little Ethiopian friend, time's near. You think we'll see anyone?"

"I hope not."

"Come on, Hodge! Don't you think it's kind of exciting?"

"No! Absolutely not!"

"All right, killer, get some sleep."

"Eat shit, Bob."

We dozed off.

Just before dawn I was roused by some unusual noises.

"Hodge, wake up. Listen. Can you hear that?"

"Yeah, it sounds like people fighting or something."

"Let's get our stuff and go."

"Bob, let's wait until light."

"No. This is what we have trained for!"

In a short time we were ready to go. As we made our way along the side of the mountain, we could hear the voices getting louder and louder.

"Hodge, how many do you think there are?"

"About five or six, I think."

"All right then. We have to make our way slowly up the hill, get to some cover, and make out what's going on. I'm afraid we're closer to the road than we think."

"SHHHH, Bob! There're lights right in front of us."

Shit! Hodge was right, and we were too close for my

liking.

"Hodge, stop here! We'll try and get closer with our ghillies on and take a look.

We put on our ghillies and started creeping along. Inch-by-inch, just like training class, we got closer and closer. The voices became more distinct. I could feel my heart pounding so loud I was afraid the bad guys could hear it, too. I gave the signal; two fingers pointed at my eyes indicated to Hodge that I saw something. As I looked through my scope, I saw two men arguing. I couldn't understand Spanish, so what they were discussing was beyond me. At this time I had no intention of shooting either one, we were way too close. A good sniper keeps his distance and waits for the optimal time, and this wasn't it. I didn't even know how many of them there were or whether Hodge would help me or not. I was sure he would... however, I had some doubt.

We watched the intersection for several days. The two individuals we had observed on the day one encounter continued to be a fixture as men and vehicles came and went. One of them, a thin, dark fellow with a bit of a pot belly and a thinning head of hair, was slightly older and appeared to be in charge of the general activities. We named him #1. The other, a younger, heavier man in a straw hat, was named #2. While these two were always on site, it was clear, after some observation, that they were some type of field lieutenants, not the masterminds of the operation. #1 always spoke to, or argued with, #2; #2 then went amongst the rabble of workers, pointing, yelling, threatening and directing whatever activity happened to be at hand. Apparently, we were watching the location of material or supply transfer for further distribution. What was being moved, we were left to guess.

On the third day, Hodge and I crawled into our location and waited for what seemed an eternity. The usual cast of characters arrived on location. Suddenly, a huge argument broke out. We had witnessed this before, but this one seemed to be on a larger scale that the previous disagreements. #1 yelled and screamed at #2, #2 ran back and forth yelling orders, directions, and curses. After a few minutes of this commotion, all activity stopped. We continued our observation, waiting for the men to do something, but nothing happened. Finally, everyone got into Jeeps and trucks and left. We waited, anticipating a return, but the area appeared to be abandoned. Hodge and I decided to creep up and investigate the location to see what all the commotion was all about.

Inching slowly, we closed the distance in about forty-five minutes. When we finally arrived we found nothing in the area but a flat tire on the ground.

"Hodge, all that commotion and its over a flat tire? Let's move away from here and get out of the low country. Make our way up to the peak and wait."

"You can't wait for an opportunity, can you, Bob?"

"No. I guess I want the chance. That's what we came here to do. Let's go."

We had been forwarded Intel on the surrounding area. We were headed for a mountaintop that was supposed to have an unobstructed view of the intersection. It was about 0900 hours when we finally made it to the top of the peak, and the view from the mountaintop was exactly the way it had been described. You could see the intersection. It was an excellent attack point. As I looked down I could see the main road running the border from east to west. It was a perfect spot with lots of brush and foliage for cover. I cut out my loophole (a hole in a bush), making sure to cut in front of the loophole to ensure fire from my weapon would not move the grass or bushes in front of the muzzle and give my position away. Odd as it sounds, it is very easy to spot something that moves fast, like grass being blown from muzzle fire. This is why snipers move slowly — detection is tougher to pick up. Satisfied I had properly prepped my position, I helped Hodge set up his spotter's position and I lay down to wait for a shot.

"Hodge, it's time. Think anyone else has done anything yet?"

"Oh, I'm sure. Open season on drug dealers?"

It wasn't too long before we started to see occasional traffic on the road, most of it going east to west. The question was, how do we know the drug dealers and gun runners? We had our suspicions from our previous observations, but no concrete evidence. Several vehicles came by, but there was no sign of the group we had been watching for the past several days. Intel had guided us to the road we were watching. Listed as a main supply route, we were set up on one of the prime ones to watch. We were also generally informed as to what type of transports they would drive. Some may be military-looking vehicles, as we had observed, and since the Honduran army was to be nowhere in the area, we wouldn't be mistaken. The lack of uniforms would also be a clear signal.

About 1800 hrs, a man holding a radio appeared, walking up the road from the south. It was #1. As he approached the intersection we could see him looking both ways and talking into his radio.

"Hodge, something's going down. This is it."

"Does look a little weird, doesn't it?"

About 10 minutes after #1 reached the intersection, a Jeep appeared with a big fat man in the front passenger's seat. The Jeep stopped and #2 hopped out of the back. It appeared very clear that the rotund man was the one in charge by the way he was maneuvering hand gestures, and the fixation he held on #1 and #2 when he spoke. We dubbed him "El Heffe." #1 was talking into the radio again.

"Hodge, this is it. We gotta to take the shot and take him out."

"Get a fix, Finger. I'll get one too."

I looked through the Mil-dot and made the quick

calculation.

"Seven hundred twenty-five yards, Hodge."

"Roger that. Confirm 725 yards. Little wind, left to right. Make the correction."

I quickly made the elevation correction and a slight correction for a left impact.

"Finger, hold a sec and let's see what else comes up the road."

I lay looking through my scope and waiting for the moment of opportunity. The fat man sitting in the old Willis Jeep was about to meet Gabriel (my weapon). To my surprise, El Heffe exited the Jeep and was yelling at #1 who was behind the Jeep talking on the radio. El Heffe, still yelling at #1, proceeded to urinate. I was polite and waited for him to finish. I had decided to wait until he sat back in the Jeep to take the shot. I wanted him stationary. As he walked back to take his seat, a flat-bed truck with a tarp cover pulled into the intersection. Several men, whom we had not seen before, jumped out of the truck. #1 and #2 immediately walked over to the truck and pulled back a corner of the tarp. The cargo was unmistakable. Wooden crates — light arms. We had watched the drugs being transferred during our previous encounters, and now part of the payoff was being collected. El Heffe sat back in the Jeep.

"Hodge?"

"You got him, Finger?"

"Got 'em."

"Give me a slight left and send it."

The explosion went off immediately, like so many times at the range.

I don't know who was more surprised by the act of violence, Hodge, me, or El Heffe, but one thing was certain, the man wouldn't be giving any more orders. The 7.62 round shattered through the windshield and penetrated his chest nearly dead center. The others, after a short lapse, started running for cover to avoid a similar fate. #1, who had sat down in the front seat, jumped out of the Jeep and hid on the side. #2 was lying flat on the ground behind the Jeep.

"Hodge, let's get the rest!"

"Negative! Absolutely not! We'll give away our position!"

Hodge's answer was sound. Generally, with one shot and the confusion that comes afterward, it is difficult to determine where the shot came from. Fire twice and your target can zero in on your location.

"We'll be okay if we get 'em all! Hodge, its now or never. You can shoot too, you know! I am going to start our little war right now. Are you with me?"

"I am not ready to do this yet."

"Fine, I'll do it myself, but if they get away, they're sure to come looking for us and kill us both!"

I put my rifle back into action. Hodge took out the guy driving the other vehicle, but it must have been a gut shot because he jumped out of the vehicle and started crawling. There appeared to be at least five of them. Some were shooting randomly at our hill. #1 was still on the side of the Jeep. I sent a round down range that hit the man in the shoulder. I ejected the spent round and for a split second, saw him look up at me before the round whistled through the air to send him to his death. By this time, the driver of the second truck, wounded in the stomach, was lying next to the Jeep, giving me a chance for leg shot. I squeezed another round off, missing his leg. The shot must have rattled him, because he started to try and crawl to the ditch. All that was exposed was his upper torso.

"Shoot, Hodge! Shoot before he hits cover!"

"Please."

That's all I needed to hear. Immediately another shot sounded. I could envision the vortex going through the evening air. The round hit him like sledge hammer. He laid his head back as his eyes focused on his last sight. Man and life met their end.

In all the excitement, #2 and a couple of others had managed to get into the big truck and it started to roll. I tried to take out the driver, but missed. That was it. They were leaving and we let some of them live. Now we were in trouble. I thought, *At least we got some of them and by the time they get back here, we will be long gone.*

Hodge took the pictures and we sat in silence looking at what had just taken place.

"Hodge, we need to leave."

We picked up our ammo, supplies, and spent rounds, and moved on in silence. We must have moved at least two miles before Hodge spoke to me.

"Where are we going?"

"I don't know, Hodge. I am just trying to put some distance behind us and get somewhere to rest and think about what just happened."

"Do you think we ought to check the map? Maybe find out where we should go so we don't get lost in the dark?"

"Yeah, you are probably right. I guess I am not thinking too clearly. My blood is pumping so hard that I can't slow down to think."

We stopped in a ravine that had a nice little creek. You could hear all kinds of peaceful sounds.

"All right, Hodge, give us our grid coordinates and let's find out where we are on the map."

He studied the map. "We are right next to the road that truck went up, Finger."

"But, there is no way. We've been heading north."

"Yes, but so is the truck."

"Okay. Well, that's a new thought. How close do you think we are to the road?"

"I would say about 200 yards."

"Let's eat and get the hell out of here. We need to make some distance. I am not so sure that they won't send

53

someone to look for us. Let's eat and make tracks."

For the next few minutes neither of us talked. We just ate in silence — or more accurately, I ate while Hodge sulked.

"Bob, you ready to go?"

"Yeah, let's get the hell out of here."

We studied our map and found a spot that looked like a good place for an ambush. It was on the El Salvador side, about five miles over the border coming into a crossroad to Honduras. It looked like the best spot for a good observation point. Intelligence said this was one of their prime roads of travel. The only downfall was that it was about 20 miles from where our current location was.

"Hodge, I think we should lie low for a day or two. Let things die down and get back to normal."

"That's the best news I've heard yet."

So we traveled for about another two or three miles and bedded down for the night.

"Hodge, can you sleep?"

"No."

"Me either. Do you feel guilty?"

"I don't know what to feel right now. To be honest with you, I just want this to be over with and go home."

"Then what?"

"I want to go to school. Maybe be a teacher or something."

"You're such a pussy. This is what you are. Live with it."

"You're wrong. I did what I set out to accomplish. Now that's over. I can go home and be at peace, if possible. I am sure this isn't for me anymore."

"Whatever. At least you took a shot. I thought for a minute you were going to puss out on me."

"I might have taken the shot, but you killed him."

"Oh, I see! So you are off the hook? Poor guy with a bullet in his stomach, will not die in agony! He'll be okay! I

54

just finished the job. You killed him the moment you put the bullet in his gut. Get some sleep. I'm tired of fighting with you. 'Night, killer."

"Shut up! You're the murderer, not me. I did it because my country ordered it. Your doing it for the infamous Finger rush — like everything else you do."

"Well, nice talking to you. See you in the morning. You're in one of your moody spells."

The next day came and went. We moved slowly to our next objective, saying nothing to each other. I felt alone on this crusade. Within about two miles from our objective, we heard gunfire and people screaming. We put on our ghillie suits and made our way toward the noise. There were about six rounds of gunfire, and that seemed to be the last of it. Then the laughter came as it echoed throughout the jungle. Hodge and I slithered our way closer and closer until I could almost feel their breath on my face. When they came into focus, what I saw was *not* the sight I expected. A big, dark-haired, mustached man had executed two men. While he was waving his pistol around he was telling people something that we couldn't understand.

"Hodge, what do you think?"

"Wait, wait…we're much too close. Besides, there are at least five of them."

"Listen, they're going to be all over me, so you are going to help me or I am going to die? Are you with me or not?"

"Yeah, I'm with you."

"I will go for the big mustached man first. After that, just pick and shoot."

I started backtracking and circling around so I was behind them about 50 yards. I couldn't get any farther away with all the trees and foliage around. So I laid my sights on the man and prayed that Hodge was going to back me up. I looked at Hodge through my scope. He was looking back at me giving me the signal — send it.

I put the sights back on again and I felt the sweat run down my face. I knew this was too close and combat was about to commence. I felt my finger slide over the trigger and slowly started pulling. The shot fired and blood splattered through the man's back onto the ground. The big man dropped to his knees and fell face first into the dirt. I immediately ejected the round and put another in the chamber. I put my sight on a smaller man looking right at me with his gun pointing in another direction. I pulled the trigger and watched him fall to the side. Then, suddenly, I was getting sprayed with bullets. All I could think of was, where was Hodge? I heard a single gunshot and all the firing stopped briefly. Hodge had taken the shooter out. I regained my composure. One man started running at me. I stood up, ready to shoot. He caught a glimpse of me and was so startled that one would have thought he'd seen Bigfoot. I think the ghillie suit scared him more than anything. He started screaming, running in another direction, until I heard that single shot again. He fell to the ground. I looked around for the last of the bunch.

I knew there was still one more, but where was he? The only thing I could do was go find him and hope that Hodge would keep a good look out for me. I started for the truck, thinking the man was hiding inside of it. As I walked up I could hear my heart pounding, yet the excitement was overwhelming. My adrenaline was pumping like crazy. I pulled out my 9MM and started for the truck. When I reached it, I opened the door from the wrong side, just in case he started shooting me. I heard nothing. I backed up and walked slowly in order to see inside the vehicle. There on the floor was the man I was looking for. I motioned for him to get up. After he got out of the truck I motioned for Hodge to come in. I made the man stand up against the truck and indicted to him not to move. Hodge came over.

"We can't let him live. We're not even supposed to be here."

To my surprise, the man answered in English.

"I never saw you! Please let me go, I won't say anything! I have a wife and children! I will tell you anything you want to know! Just don't!"

I started the interrogation. I asked about the men who were executed. He told us that they had been caught stealing from their boss. They had been instructed to take them to the border and execute them.

"Exactly what did they take?"

"Cocaine. The people who work for him are not allowed to even have the habit! He would kill you if you stole from him. He wants only people that want to make money and do not have a drug habit."

I thought of the irony. Drug addiction keeps people buying drugs, yet the drug dealer didn't want his own people addicted. I guess he realized what crap it is and the things that it does to the mind.

"So, what do you have in your vehicle?"

"Nothing! We just came out here to do this and go back."

"Go back where?"

"Please! I can't tell you that! He will kill me and my whole family!"

"What do you think we are going to do to you?"

He pointed to a place on the map. I figured any information we could get out of him and report back to the base would help our cause. I asked him to tell me all the places of interest on the map, and if he hesitated, he would be shot like the others. He showed us all the places that he knew on the map. When he finished, I told him if he had lied to us in any way, he would take the first bullet. He thanked us many times for sparing him, and he took off.

"Well, Hodge, what do you think?"

"We just signed our death warrant."

"Why?"

"What? You think they are just going stand by and let

this happen without retaliation? They're going to kill him first, and then come after us! Someone is coming out here to find us and kill us! Rest assured!"

"We're better trained, well supplied, and we've got good Intel. Surely we can get them before they get us."

"Not on this side of the border. We gotta to get back to safety. We gotta get back closer to home."

"Okay. Let's get the hell out of here and finish up."

Hodge and I crossed back to the other side of the border. Back to safety, if that's what you could call it. We walked until nightfall. When we finally stopped for the night, it seemed all too quick before the sun was rising. The next day came and went while we moved to our next location. Most of the time, moving through the jungle was like walking by myself. Hodge seemed to be lost in his own thoughts. He didn't care to talk to me unless I directed a question to him. Other than that, it was silence for two entire days of walking. I guess I don't blame him. I'm sure he blamed me for everything that had happened. I personally didn't care all that much. I was doing what was asked of me. I was a soldier. Hodge would just have to live with that.

I felt as though my life was changing with every moment and with every step. The hatred I felt was becoming much worse — not hatred toward anybody in particular, but the hatred over the meanness that was enveloping me, and how the situation was creating this meanness in me. I couldn't stop thinking of how it felt to shoot another human being. It was unbelievable, both a thrill and a curse. I had reoccurring questions. Was what I did right? Was it wrong? The same answer floated in and out of my mind. *Kill them all! You are a soldier! You are doing your country a great service.* The feeling of killing another man was something I have never felt before. I liked it. The problem I could see starting to show its face was being able to quit. It's hard to understand unless you have experienced it. It was a rush.

"Bob, you know we are going to Hell for this,"

Hodge said.

"Do you think he'll need snipers too, Hodge?"

"You're demented! What's wrong with you? Don't you feel any remorse for what just happened? Any mercy?"

"I have mercy. I let the man live, didn't I?"

"You just don't get it, do you?"

"Quit your bellyaching. I don't want to shoot you, too!" I began to laugh.

"That thought has crossed my mind. You probably would, if there weren't anyone else."

"Hodge, you're a puss! Let's just get the hell out of here and go back to the drop zone. I'll finish this myself. Go! Get the hell out of here! You make me sick! I am tired of all this crying shit."

"Come on, I didn't say I wouldn't help! I just need someone to talk to, and you don't make it very easy."

"You're my friend and my spotter. If you need to talk to justify your actions, go ahead."

"Maybe I have been an ass. I am a sensitive man," I said with a sarcastic laugh.

For the next day or so, Hodge and I talked about the events of the past couple days; how each of us felt about it. It was two clearly different takes on the whole mess. Hodge really did feel guilty. He considered his soul condemned. He thought he was going to Hell. I thought of myself as the crusader for the country and I wanted to do everything I could to save it. We'd been in the mix now for a little over a week. Several men had died because of our intervention — or more accurately, *my* intervention. Regardless, they were dead. I knew one thing with certainty; I was getting itchy for more.

The travel to the next location was unbearable. The underbrush was so thick it made it almost impossible to move. Making matters worse, we were running a little thin on food and water. The food drop was about 30 miles away and wasn't scheduled for three more days. Our next objective was a trail that had been marked for foot travel. From what we were told, vehicles were parked nearby and runners went into the area on horseback. We were about 13 miles from their trail.

"Bob, should we bed down for the night and try to hit the area in the morning?"

"Yeah, I guess. You know, we'll still have quite a hike in the morning. I know what you're up to."

"What would that be?"

"Stalling, Hodge. I say we move until we only have a little farther to go so we can set up camp, and then wait for our next opportunity."

"However you want. That's the way it always is, isn't it?"

I grunted and started ahead. We made our way up the hill and came across a road where people were standing. We were caught off guard because of our little feud. At first we just stood there looking at each other for what seemed an eternity. There were four of them looking at us with the obvious question on their faces: What the hell are you doing here? By their reactions, I could tell they had heard Hodge and I arguing. Now we were caught with them looking right at us.

I did what I thought was best. I waved to them. One of them waved back and started telling one of the others something. Most of them were well armed. I waited for them to make the first move. One slowly moved his hand to his rifle. I told Hodge they were going for their weapons. We were about 50 yards from them. Without thinking I raised my rifle and sent a bullet down range. Chaos ensued and bullets started flying everywhere. The men ran behind a junk car. Hodge and I got down and tried to get into cover.

"What the hell are you doing?"

"Hodge, they were going for their weapons! I'm not going to just stand there and take automatic weapon fire! We gotta kill 'em, or we die!"

I tried to move down the ravine a little to get a shot. In the meantime, the four locals were spraying bullets everywhere. I could see the top of one of their heads through the glass of the vehicle. I shot, but to my surprise, missed. How I could have missed so close? It must have been the adrenaline. And where the hell was Hodge? Looking under the vehicle, I could see the bad guys on their knees behind it. I took a shot of opportunity and hit one in the knee. He fell to the side and I heard Hodge fire a shot to finish him off. Finally! During all the commotion, I noticed two others running into the woods on the other side of the road. I took aim and shot. The round struck one of them in the back and I watched him fall face-first into the dirt. While I was reloading, the second one was getting away. I couldn't leave any witnesses this time.

I ran up to the car, pulled out my 9mm and shot each of the men again to ensure they were dead. Then I started after the one headed into the jungle. I ran into the trees for a while, then stopped, closed my eyes, and listened. I could hear branches breaking about 75 yards ahead of me. I took off — and in doing so, I committed an unforgivable sin. I left my partner. At the time I couldn't have cared less. I had only one thing on my mind — I had to track and kill the last one.

After an hour or so I spotted him sitting next to a tree. It appeared that he was wiping his forehead. I raised my weapon for a shot, but something came over me. Instead of a final blow, I shot his rifle in the receiver section, disabling it. He was weaponless, and now I could hunt him like an animal. The chase was back on. I tracked and chased him for about another half mile. When I caught up to him, he was trying to climb a tree. I shot him in the leg. He fell to the ground and started to crawl. I strapped my rifle around my shoulder and armed myself with the 9mm. I wanted a close-up shot. I approached him and saw nothing but fear in his eyes. As I sat there looking at him, he didn't seem as brave as he once had. I loved the feeling of power. He started to say something to me, which I couldn't understand and didn't really care to. I raised my pistol and shot him.

I looked into his pockets and found a souvenir. In retrospect, it was the behavior some serial killers display toward their victims. I found a coin and some money, and I took it. Part of me felt like a no-good piece of crap, akin to a sort of criminal. Shooting a guy and then robbing him? This wasn't the mindset that I had. I just wanted something to remember him by. Regardless, his life was over and mine was about to be turned upside down. I was just too stupid to see it. I headed back to the road, hoping to calm Hodge down.

Chapter 6
Finding Hodge

When I arrived at the scene of the firefight, Hodge was nowhere to be found. I headed back up the mountain to get back to the agreed upon rally point. (A rally point is designated place of return if you are separated from your partner.) After about an hour, I made it there. No Hodge. I thought, *What the hell? Where is he?* I decided to eat something and wait for him. The night came and went, still no Hodge. As I sat there, thoughts began racing through my mind. *I'm alone now! It's my fault for leaving him! What the fuck!* I couldn't sleep the whole time.

Next morning I went back to the site of the massacre by a different route. As I approached over the hill, I saw two more vehicles. Eight men were looking over the scene. I stayed very quiet, put on my ghillie, sat down and observed. Then I saw something I wish I hadn't. Someone picked up one of the spent 9mm rounds that I'd forgotten to police. Damn! What was I thinking! This was a cardinal sin! Never, *ever* leave any trace of being there! This way, there is no trace back to American forces in the area. Sniper rounds for rifles are sometimes different than those of ordinary rounds, which would surely give us away. I had probably jeopardized our situation by letting them know Americans were in the area. This was a 9mm round I had been in too damn much of a hurry to pick up. I had lost control of the situation.

Where the hell was Hodge? I started to get very worried and angry wondering why he left me. Then I realized that *I* had left *him*. Damn! He had the global positioning unit (GPS) and the map with all the projected enemy targets. I did have a map, but it would not help me in completing the mission. Who the hell was I kidding? Without Hodge, the mission was over, and I was in deep shit.

I sat and watched as another vehicle approached. It appeared to be some kind of vehicle to transport bodies, probably live, not dead. Several men from the vehicles started loading up the bodies. In the meantime, another started shouting and pointing all over the place. He looked pissed. After the bodies were loaded, the crowd finally left the scene. It was probably around 1400 hours until the coast was clear, and there was still no sign of Hodge.

I decided to go back to the rally point, hoping Hodge had shown up while I was gone. I reached it after a couple of hours and looked for signs of him. There was nothing. I was starting to get scared. What the hell! The last thing I needed was my head playing games with me. I started to think those guys were Hondurans and not El Salvadorians. Maybe I made a mistake…shot the wrong people? Maybe there were more people in the woods and they took Hodge. I was driving myself nuts. I had to quit this, continue on and find him. There was no way Hodge could have gotten caught. I would have heard a shot or something. I decided to go back to the road to see if I could pick up his trail and maybe find him. Unfortunately, he had a big head start, and I was worried about his mental condition, even though mine was a wreck right now.

I arrived back at the site where I had last seen Hodge. I could see no rounds or imprints of them. It would appear that Hodge had never even shot. I knew he'd shot once, but unlike me, he'd cleaned his plate. As I looked and dug closer, I could see slight imprints the dirt the more horizontal I got to the ground. It appeared he had headed into the trees across the road to follow me. Hodge wasn't the best tracker in the world. It was possible he was lost. I tracked his prints for about an hour. It was very tedious and time-consuming, but what the hell else did I have to do? I lost his track, and after that, couldn't find it again. From the signs of Hodge's tracks, he appeared to be wandering all over the place. There was no consistent pattern to which direction he was traveling. This was not out of character for snipers. We were taught very early in our career to never follow an easy path, and most of all, show no signs of direction, even if that meant backtracking or clearing your path to hide your trail. Well, Hodge was doing something right, because I lost him and couldn't find anything.

There is a special trick trackers use when they can't find the next track. Get a stick, and measure the person's stride. When you lose the track, lay the stick on the ground and move it in a 180° angle sweeping motion. You should find the next track in line. Unfortunately, this tactic didn't work this time. I started using the circle technique, another tracking tool. You start by going 10-20 feet in the circle of the last impression of what you are tracking, looking for a sign that wasn't covered. I found nothing. I moved out 40 feet, and low and behold, I found a newly broken branch. I picked up his trail again. Where the hell was he going? Then it dawned on me. He was cutting right across my mess of a trail. Hodge was on it! He was looking for me, and he was alive and well! When I was tracking the guy in the woods, I hadn't covered up anything. I made a big highway showing where I had been.

What followed next was mind-boggling. I came upon the scene of my trophy. At first glance it appeared the man had left! The man I killed was...gone! I had left him right by a tree, and I knew he was dead. I put too many rounds in him for him to have lived. I looked closer. The body had been buried. Hodge must have found him and buried him. But why? Hodge was losing it. To hell with this guy! The coyotes could have him. Maybe Hodge was trying to cover our tracks, or...was he feeling remorse? I didn't know the answer.

Finding the grave was very disturbing to me. Hodge had lost it. Now I had to find him. Would Hodge try to kill me? Maybe I pushed him over the edge of sanity. I began tracking Hodge again. For about two miles it was easy tracking. He appeared to be going to our destination on the trail. I kept moving slowly, expecting to hear a lone gunshot, and then I would find him.

After the day came to a close with no visual contact of Hodge, I decided to fire a shot into the air to see if Hodge would answer. I fired a single round. Nothing. He either didn't want me with him anymore, or he was dead. I didn't know, but my status of crusader was fading fast. I started to get scared. I was becoming lonely without my friend.

I bedded down for the night and lay thinking about what would happen to me when I got back to the states and Hodge, my spotter, my friend, wasn't with me. Would I be blamed? Would someone think I murdered my friend? I lay all night in the jungle thinking about Hodge. I was beginning to feel very lonely, then suddenly I heard what sounded like a shot in the air. My mind raced. Was that Hodge...or the enemy? Did Hodge take his own life? I fired a shot back. I didn't care at this point. *Come and find me, Hodge, or whoever you are!* I thought.

Silence followed and an eerie feeling came over me. I began to have depressing thoughts. My morale began to sink. I had hit the iceberg. I started to believe Hodge was dead. The enemy had murdered him, or he had committed suicide. I realized that I was now really alone. The feeling overtook over my whole being. It was not what I would have expected. Anger began rolling through my veins; anger and the thirst for blood. I convinced myself that the enemy had murdered Hodge, and I wanted revenge. It was very likely I just needed something to focus on besides my own mistakes.

When morning came, I was on the prowl to the destination from where the shot had originated. After a few hours, I arrived to find nothing. I looked in my scope for hours, hoping to see Hodge out there. He had to be there! I heard the shot. I felt like standing up and screaming his name.

Lost in my thoughts, I suddenly noticed 10 men walking with mules as they entered my sight coming up the trail. I sat staring at them. My thoughts turned to a single focus. They had killed my friend, now was time to pay them back. I knew they would kill me, but I didn't care. They were vermin, and I needed to slaughter them. I didn't care if I was alone. I was going to kill them all. The rage I felt was unimaginable. There was still a little seed of hope in my mind. If Hodge was still alive, he would back me up. Rage and fury overcame my thoughts. All I could picture was Hodge's death. All I wanted was revenge so I could soothe my rage and frustration. It was time to go hunting.

Like a tiger stalking its prey, I waited for the enemy to come into the open. The first shot echoed through the trees, and to my surprise, I missed! They stood frozen and stunned. No wonder they didn't scatter. They didn't even realize they were taking fire!

"I never miss! My mind is not where it needs to be! I am a mess. All right, get yourself together and do it right!"

I didn't care if they all scattered and disappeared into the jungle. I would track each one down and kill them. Hell's messenger was descending on them and wrath was coming. I put my sights on an open target. This time the bullet hit its mark.

"Not a good shot. Looks like I hit him in the waist. What the hell is wrong with you?" I chastised myself.

Finally the enemy reacted. They started spraying bullets all around me. The fight was beginning and I was the winning team. I enjoyed watching the suffering, the flowing of blood, and the carnage. I felt like a wrathful god, punishing the wicked. I could see them out of every corner of my eye, trying to find me. Now the game began. I would only take shots that counted.

The rules of the game suddenly changed. I noticed the enemy fanning out and moving up the hill in an attempt to surround me. Logic came back. It was time to get the hell out of here. I threw away the idea of trying to take them all. I needed to work my way out and stay alive. This group was very organized and they appeared to have been expecting me. Instead of trying to run away, they began to track me.

I knew one thing for sure — Hodge wasn't out there. I had a bunch of people on my ass and I had to get out — fast! I ghillied up and started to move. I made my way back into deepest part of the jungle. I found a tree that had been rotted out, dug some of it out, camouflaged myself into the tree and took up roots. I tried to cover my route and make myself disappear.

After an hour or so of hiding in my nest, I realized I was no longer alone. I could hear voices around my position. I was screwed! If they found me, I couldn't do anything tightly fitted into the tree. All they had to do was shoot the tree and I was dead.

Where the hell is Hodge? Why did I hide in this damn tree?

What happened next nearly stopped my heart. One of my pursuers sat on the dead tree where I was hidden. He sat there for an eternity, talking to his comrade. I could hear my own breath. I could hear my heart pounding, and I was close to my wit's end. Bugs crawled over me and giant wood ants bit my legs. I thought death might almost be better than the torture I was experiencing at that moment. I wasn't very religious, but I recall praying to God to please get me out of this. I felt a giant bug crawling up my pants leg. The feeling was awful. I almost couldn't take it any longer when, suddenly, the man sitting on the tree got up and start walking away.

I waited about twenty minutes and slowly crawled out of the log. I brushed myself off, took off my pants, and swatted the bugs away. I looked at my legs, now covered with numerous insect bites. Some were extremely painful and were beginning to swell into large welts. I started back on the move. This time I headed back toward the drop zone. I needed food, water, and ammo. Most of all, I hoped to find my friend there, although my hopes weren't too high. I had enough food for two days, if I ate sparingly, and I estimated it would take me about four to five days to get back. I just wanted to get back and find Hodge. I didn't care about the mission anymore. I missed my friend. I wanted to go home. I was prepared to face the wrath of the board.

Trying to reach the drop zone was going to be difficult. First, I didn't have the GPS unit. Second, my map wasn't marked out very well with points. One thought did come to mind — if I could kill one of the trackers and take their supplies, I could survive a few more days and make it out. Finding one of my tormentors was the key to my survival. Well, not *really*, I could live off the land. But, who wants to?

Slowly working my way through the jungle, I came upon a man sitting over a log, apparently taking a morning crap. His weapon sat next to him, slightly out of reach. This would be an easy take, and he might have been one of the men chasing me. Now the question: Take his life or move on? It was now or never. I decided I had done enough killing. It was time for me to move on, even if he presented an easy target. I could have had some water and possibly food, but I couldn't find it in my heart to kill him. I slipped by him unnoticed, and moved on.

I started making my way through the brush trying to find the drop zone. My compass was a great help, but I was starting to get confused using the map. I couldn't identify which mountain was which. Panic was starting to creep into my mind. Not only did I have to deal with being lost, but also I wondered if my friend was lost as well… or dead.

"Damn it! You're losing your grip!"

I started to think that Hodge had taken his own life. I started to believe that he was dead. If not, he should have found me by now. He would have been at the rally point or the next location of opportunity. He hadn't been, and I was alone in Hell.

I spent the next day trying to make my way back, still fearing that I was lost. Nothing appeared to be familiar. A horrible feeling of hopelessness began to infect my mind. I thought my friend had deserted me. None of the mountains looked familiar. I had to find something positive. That something was my old trusty compass. In dense jungle it's hard to keep on course, especially without a GPS. I could not pinpoint my location with the map and a compass. So, I kept heading west, attempting to find something that looked familiar.

Evening approached too quickly, and I still found myself alone. I was scared and lost. As I settled in for the night, I kept thinking over and over about what had happened to my missing friend. My food was running out. I didn't even know where exactly the drop zone was. I did know one thing for sure — I had two weeks before I was going home. I guessed my mission was over. I had no camera, no Hodge, no radio, no idea what the next objective was, and I was lost. For all I knew, I was in El Salvador. Without fail, I had to avoid all personnel.

I woke to the sound of gunfire. It was about 0300. What the hell was that? How far away was it? Was it Hodge? I had to go and find out, to see if by some chance it was Hodge. I packed up and started on the move toward the sound of the gunfire. After an hour of traveling, I had heard nothing. I didn't have a clue which way I should proceed. I knew I was heading south, either farther in or toward the earlier gunfire, but not the direction I needed to go to reach the drop zone. I kept going until my ears caught the sounds someone talking. It was Hodge! I heard one shot. I found myself going faster and faster toward the location of the shot.

I had to cautiously pick my way through the jungle —it was dense and I couldn't move too fast. And it was dark. The overhead vegetation was thick and concealed the moonlight.

I was rolling with adrenaline. I moved slowly through the thick vegetation up a lonely ridge. As I looked at the ridge, I thought of how ironic it was that this was a perfect place for a sniper to lay out. The problem I now faced was I could no longer hear any voices or gunfire. What was going on? Where the hell was I?

I stopped and stayed still for a while. The sun would be up in less than an hour. Then, I could see where I was and what was happening. As dawn approached, I was still unable see much, if anything. There still was no sound of gunfire, and no sound of men talking. The jungle was eerily devoid of any sounds whatsoever. I decided to start moving again, this time heading west in an attempt to pinpoint my location. The thought occurred to me that if I headed south and found the border road, I could follow the road up to the drop zone. Then I would know exactly where I was. I changed course and headed south toward the border road and prayed that I hadn't already gone too far.

I moved throughout the day, but located no distinct road. I found lots of roads, just not the one I considered a major border road. I was getting really confused. I figured I had gone about five miles south and still nothing looked familiar. I set out, heading west again, trying to find a landmark.

As had become custom, night came all too fast. I came to the realization I was completely lost. The feeling of being lost in a country like El Salvador was scary. I didn't know anyone, nor could I speak the language. I lay in my bag wondering how I had gotten myself into such a predicament, with wild thoughts going through my head.

This is God's way of punishing me for doing all the horrible things that I did, not the least of which dragging

around Hodge making him party to it. I should be shown some mercy, right? I did let the one guy go, didn't I?

Who was I kidding? I didn't even believe in God.

I started to blame Hodge.

He's the reason I am lost and confused. He deserted me. He knew the plans for separations and he failed to follow through. Now I'm in this lonely isolated place.

Being alone was the worst feeling in the world. I was mad as hell at Hodge, but I would hug him to death if I ever saw him again. This time we would just be on vacation. Take it easy. No more hero crap. It'd just be me and him, hanging out in the jungle. I loved Hodge. He was my friend. He was like my brother. I missed him terribly.

All through the night I heard noises; bugs chirping, spiders crawling through the grass, movements of the trees, and yet the worst of all was the dead silence. Silence made me think too much. Silence gives a person time to think about his life and what he may have to answer for. The thought of dying was now becoming more and more a real possibility to me.

Morning came too early, and I had hardly slept. I figured it was time to get myself out of this shithole. I looked for the highest peak and headed for it. Now the only problem was that my food and water supplies were running out. I could get water from the streams, but we had been warned about drinking the possibly disease-infested water. I thought about trying to build a condensation still to make some drinking water, but that would probably take time I didn't have to spare. The only thing for certain was the mountain was getting higher and I was getting thirstier.

Finally, I reached the top and found a nice lookout. From this vantage point, I looked through my scope for some sign of life. Then it happened! There is a God! I found the road that I was looking for. It had to be the road. Now, which way to go? Was I too far down or too far up? I had to be too far down. Common sense told me that. Now was the time to make some decisions. My only problem was I couldn't come up with any. Was I far enough up the road, or not? I was lost. I needed to find the mountain where we had our first encounter. I looked at every mountain in view. They all looked the same. I estimated I was about one mile off the road. Now that I had the road in sight, I wasn't going to leave it again.

I began to hike, paralleling the road, and trying to find something that looked familiar. I was now out of water, and had no idea where I was — but, I had the road. Now I felt better inside. After hiking for an hour or so, I decided I needed water no matter what disease it may contain. I started to sing to myself, "A hiking I will go, a hiking I will go, and water I will find..." The things we do to entertain ourselves in times of distress.

Relief came about two hours later. I found a nice, stale pond that looked like a grease trap. What do you do when you're out of water and dying of dehydration? I could boil the water and take the chance of someone seeing the smoke. No thanks. I took off my shirt, filled it water, using my shirt as a filter to catch the debris and filled my canteens with lovely, murky crap. I dropped in a few water purifying tablets and about an hour later, I decided I'd drink the disgusting swill. I would have never guessed it, but it tasted pretty good. Of course, sour milk would have tasted good by this time. I refilled the canteen, put in a few more tablets, and started on my way again.

Everything started getting a little better. I had plenty of water, now that I discovered I could make water from disgusting puddles and ponds. All I needed was Hodge. Finding the drop zone would be a nice benefit, too. I felt my positive mindset getting stronger. I started heading down the side of the road, keeping it about a mile off to my left.

It was getting late, and I was starving. I wasn't hungry enough to eat worms or anything of that nature yet;

however, if I saw some small animal, I thought I might trap or shoot it. No, maybe not. I didn't want to give my position away and I didn't have time to set snares. I decided to I'd have to make my way back to the DZ and get supplies.

I found a good place to lie down and call it a night. I gathered up some leaves and branches — anything that was soft — and built myself a nice, comfortable bed. I laid down my sleeping bag, put my weapon down beside me, and made sure that my position on the side of the hill was nice and secluded. Now for some sleep. Tomorrow I would find Hodge and the DZ. Of course, negative thoughts crept into my mind. *What if I don't find Hodge? What I am going to do then?* I had to think positive. Hodge was still alive. The DZ was just right over the hill. *I hate insomnia. I need to go to sleep and stop worrying.*

When morning came, I was lying in the bag starving and wondering if food was over the hill. I couldn't think anything but food. Burger King, pizza, anything. *I would die for Taco Bell!*

One thing was certain, I was thinking now of killing anyone on the road just to look for food or something else to drink. No women or children, just the usual criminals. I was fantasizing about finding food. I didn't really need to kill someone for it. I could live off the land. I was just being spoiled and didn't want the work of catching it. Nonetheless, I was out to try and get some easy food and water. I had the mindset that all men were evil. If I killed them, they probably deserved it anyway. If someone were to kill me, I knew I deserved it. I knew I wasn't thinking clearly. I was rambling on, but that happens when your body and mind are under great stress. I knew this. I needed to talk to myself; to convince myself of the justification of my earlier actions and of those yet to come. I moved closer to the road.

It was noon. I spotted a truck sitting on the road, heading north. I wasn't sure if this was just some local person or some of our criminals. I had to investigate. I got within 300 yards of the truck and I only saw one person. *What is he doing just sitting there?*

I saw him crawl under his truck. *Ah-ha, truck problems, and he's all alone.* I came down the mountain to give him a cordial greeting. When I was within 50 yards of him, I stopped and looked through my scope to make sure the coast was clear. Sure enough, there was only this one guy. Strange thoughts forged in my head. *Should I shoot or not? Am I getting soft?*

I had to do it, just to prove I still had it in me. Strangest thing, I couldn't pull the trigger. This was the perfect opportunity. There had to be something in the truck. How could I look into the truck and not let him know I was there? I could fire a shot by him, scare him into running down the road, and then look.

I must have sat there for an hour, debating what to do, when another truck showed up. Whatever opportunity there had once been was now gone. I could kill them both, but I was in Honduras now and these two individuals were probably just locals. I left them alone. My luck proved to be holding out when both men got into the operable truck and left.

I slithered over to the broken-down truck and started looking. What I found was something that I couldn't believe; a half-empty bag of potato chips and some weird kind of cookies. I gathered my treasures, moved back to my safe position and started for the next hill in front of me.

I slowly made my way through the never-ending jungle and overgrowth until I found the perfect place to enjoy my stolen dinner. I sat, bent over a tree, and ate the most delicious chips and cookies I had ever enjoyed. In reality they probably tasted like crap, but after a while without food, this tasted like a gourmet meal. After devouring the bag of chips and every crumb of the cookies, it was time to start moving. I knew I should have saved some for later, but I couldn't stop myself.

The path I was on seemed like familiar territory. A good sign. I could swear the road to the first kill zone was just ahead, it looked so familiar. I started to get excited. The lost feeling was going away. The feeling of cockiness was returning.

I made it to the hill and I found my tracks. Now I knew exactly what mountain I was on! The DZ was within six miles or so! I have never been as happy in my life as I was at that moment. I headed to the DZ. I couldn't wait! I needed so many things — food, water, and mostly, Hodge. I was ready to leave this shithole — get back to civilization. I guessed I was about three miles out to the DZ; however, night was coming on again and this time I didn't want to take the chance of getting lost, so it was time to bed down for the night. Needless to say, it was a sleepless night.

At the first sign of light, I resumed my hike toward the DZ. My heart was pumping so fast I couldn't believe the feeling. But, within a mile of the location, I fell. In my excitement, I had not been watching my step. I twisted my ankle and the swelling and pain hit immediately. Could my luck get any worse? I thought I'd broken my ankle — and this close to the DZ. *SHIT!*

I took off my boot to look at my ankle. It didn't appear to be broken, but it was definitely twisted. I pulled my boot back on, tightened the laces as tight as I could get them, and started walking again. Now the walk was slow and painful, but I was only trying to make it another mile.

As I made my way around the mountain, I could see the location where we had jumped in. Now I was only 600 yards from my box of goodies. It took a while to get there, but I made it. I felt like a lost child finding its mother. I felt comfortable and relaxed. This was where I would stay for the rest of my time.

Inside the box of goodies I found food, water, and ammo. On closer inspection, the box appeared to have been tampered with. Hodge had been there! There was food and ammo missing. Why hadn't Hodge stayed? Why was he still out there? As far as I was concerned, this job was over. I just wanted to stay here and wait for the pick-up. My ankle was probably broken and I was out of commission. I gulped volumes of water and ate until I felt sick. I loaded up with ammo and made a nice little bed. I wasn't going anywhere. Hodge not being at the DZ ate at me. Why had he come and left? WHY? He wasn't capable of performing the mission by himself.

I decided to stay at the DZ and wait for Hodge. I couldn't walk anyway, and he would come back eventually. I started to feel lonely and remorseful for the way that I had pushed Hodge into escalating things. He hadn't been ready. I was the one that couldn't resist temptation. I don't know what came over me, but I started reminiscing about old times. I started thinking of my friends in school, my mother, and my life to date. I wondered how I got to where I was. I remembered the ridicule of my teachers. I thought of the lack of awareness that teachers have about the influence they have over children. I knew I had spent my whole life trying to prove I was important; that I mattered. I was not the loser others envisioned. I wished all the people from my past were here at this moment. Some of my teachers had been the best, it was just a few that refused to see the lost little boy that needed help and guidance that I couldn't shake.

Old times. No wonder I am the way I am. For the most part, the townspeople where I'd grown up had been arrogant, inconsiderate people. Most of my teachers were the same way. If you didn't have a name, you were nothing. What the hell was I doing protecting these people? Why should I try and defend a country made up of people with attitudes? I considered the idea of a nation obsessed with status. A prevailing notion that without social stature, you're nothing. The attitude filters down of "I'm not top-shelf, but I'm better than you." The more I thought about it, the more a picture came into focus. The people protecting the country, my brothers-in-arms, were not the graduates of the Ivy League. They were not those considered the intellectual elite. They were the poor, the commonplace. Individuals, in some circles, considered to be the trash of society. Why? Why do the ones with the least to lose defend those with the most to gain? I couldn't derive an answer, but I began to feel disgruntled.

Finally, given plenty of time to think, these thoughts came to my mind. I was mad at our society for not getting a fair shake, yet I was asked to kill for it and defend it. As a child, I was considered nothing but trash. Had I changed, or was I still the same? The government had trust in me. They spent large amounts of money training me. For the first time in my life I felt as though someone — or something — valued me. The government and the USMC were my family. They didn't treat me like a societal outcast. It was my obligation to do what they wanted. They rewarded me for bravery; decorated me with medals. They made me feel special, important, worthy. For kid that always saw life on the wrong side of the tracks, it meant a lot.

After a round of reminiscing and melancholy, I decided to stay the night and carry on with the mission, broken ankle or not. I would stay close by, and not go farther than 15 miles. That was it. Night fell and I finally got a decent night's sleep. For the first time in a long time, I felt important, loved, and needed. What else was there?

Morning came and my ankle screamed with pain. I took off my boot and inspected my swollen ankle. It looked like I'd dipped it in a container of yellow paint. I decided to rest it for a while and let it get some air. I soaked my shirt with water from my canteen and wrapped it around my ankle. I looked up at the clouds and saw a figure that looked like an angel. ***God is looking over me.*** The feeling didn't last. I really didn't believe in God. I had my reasons. *Why would God allow so many horrible things to happen, especially to a child?* I didn't know that it would make me a stronger person in the end. *Maybe we shouldn't try to understand why God does the things he does. Just try and live with them, and sooner or later you'll find out.*

About 0900 hours I heard a strange sound. I caught the sound of someone walking slowly up the ravine. I pulled my boot on as fast as I could. I grabbed my weapon and slowly moved forward. I had no idea who it was, or how many of them there might be. I could hear sound only a few seconds at a time. Then it stopped and started again. Was it Hodge? It didn't sound like more than one person. Was it someone sent to kill us? I had no idea, but one thing I knew for certain; I was a good Marine and whoever was coming was about to die.

About 60 yards from camp, I laid my weapon down and tried to get an eye on who or what was coming. I couldn't see or hear anything now. I sat for about an hour, looking intently. As my eyes searched, I noticed someone watching me through their scope. It was Hodge! I waved at him and he waved back...however, something didn't seem quite right. I wondered if he'd shoot me if I stood up. I didn't care anymore. I stood up and started to hobble back to the camp, and I saw Hodge get up and start walking toward me.

Chapter 7

Unmerciful

I never was so glad to see anyone, and yet so disappointed all in the same moment. I couldn't believe that Hodge was there. ***Where the hell have you been?*** There were questions to be answered. I slowly walked up to the camp, keeping a keen eye on my compadre. He strolled up as casually as if he were returning from the men's room. The closer I came to the camp, the more I saw of Hodge's face and the disturbing look that was on it. I needed to figure out what the hell had gone on for the last few days and where the hell he'd been.

"Hodge, what the hell? Where have you been?"

"What's wrong with your leg, Bob? Get shot?"

"No, I fell and twisted my ankle. Now, where the hell have you been?"

"Well, I went to look for you, and found the remains of your last trophy. So I decided to cover the evidence, and give the man a decent burial."

"Yeah, that's all great Hodge, then where did you go?"

"Well, I went to the next place that we had talked about."

"No, Hodge, you didn't because I was there. No thanks to you I almost died. Now, quit lying to me and tell me what the hell happened to you."

"Look, I needed some time to just get away and think."

"What? You left me so you could *think*? I should kill you! You know what the hell I've been through? I almost died! I hurt my ankle! I had to drink shit for water and I ran out of food, not to mention being lost for days!"

"I don't want to hear it, Bob. You caused it all

yourself."

"What the fuck are you talking about?"

"You're the one who had to run off and leave me. For your thrills and excitement, to get that last kill."

"That wasn't it! I didn't want him to tell anyone we were here! That's it! Now, why did you leave me? You obviously came looking for me, and then left me."

"I didn't leave you. I went back after burying your trophy, but you weren't there."

"Hodge, I went back looking for you. I stayed there waiting on you. I never would have left you. Never! You're my friend!"

"I'm sorry, Bob. I don't know what to say except I needed time to evaluate my life. If I'd stayed with you, who knows what I would have become?"

"I don't understand."

"You're a psycho, and you live for the adrenaline rush, I don't. All I ever wanted to do was measure up. You showed me that. I know now what I am capable of. That's all that matters."

"Let's forget all about it. We'll talk about it later. We've got more important things to talk about, like what are we going to do now?"

"I was thinking about finishing the mission, but your ankle is messed up."

"You mean to tell me you want to go out and do some more?"

"Yes, I want to do what I signed up for. I'm ready to carry on now. Are you up to it?"

"You know me. I am always ready for a new trophy. Know any good taxidermists?" I laughed. "Hey, let's stay here and talk for a while. Stay the night and move out in the morning. We can try and find a nice easy place to go to. Now that I'm hobbled up, I can't go too far."

Hodge sat down and ate lunch. We talked about old times. We never mentioned what had happened. We just reminisced about times at home, growing up, and joining the Corps. It was two old buddies at a reunion talking about old times. We started talking about our drill instructors and our time in ITS (Infantry Training School) where Hodge and I met, the fun we had going to Hollywood, and the partying we did.

"Bob, when we get back, you and I are going back to Hollywood and getting drunk. Maybe get laid, too!" Hodge said.

"The only way I will agree to that is if you buy me the more expensive hooker. You can have the streetwalker. I need a call girl."

"Your ass! I'm buying you one with an STD for what you put me through." He laughed. "What else are we going to do?"

"Well, we will go to the beach and do some diving. Maybe catch some lobsters. You know, Hodge, it sounds so good, but so far away."

"It's not that far, Finger. Only a week and few days left."

"Yeah, you don't think the plane could crash before we get home?"

"Weren't you the one who said quit sending me negative waves?"

"Yeah, I did say that. Let's talk about what we're going to do now."

"Just relax for the day. We'll get up tomorrow and go hunt someone for you."

"All right, Hodge. What else do you wanna talk about?"

"Do you remember when I said I wanted to be a teacher?"

"Yeah."

"Well, now I really want to be a teacher."

"Why such a big change? I mean, why so bad now?"

"I remember you saying how your teachers had so

much influence on you, even though it was mostly bad. Well, I want to give kids a chance and be a positive influence on them, even the bad ones."

"The bad ones?"

"Yeah, they're the ones that need it the most. I can make a difference now."

"Why now?"

"Look at what I have been through. I think I have matured a lot lately. The experience has helped me look at life in a whole different light. I'd like to help people instead of destroying them."

"I know what you are saying Hodge, but I can't. I just don't see people as good."

"Bob, have you ever seen the movie *Pollyanna*?"

"No, I can't say that I have."

"Well, in the movie Pollyanna tells a preacher a little verse from Abraham Lincoln. It goes like this: If you look for the evil in man you will surely find it."

"So, what you are trying to tell me is that I look for evil, not good?"

"Yep."

"Maybe I do look for the bad. You could be right. But I've never known much good. People always want something from you. No one does things without wanting something in return, and generally with an underhanded way of getting it."

"That's not true, Bob. There are good people out there. And good friends. Let me tell you a quote: A friend is like an enemy in disguise."

"What the hell is that supposed to mean?" I asked.

"Okay, if someone that doesn't know you hates you, do you care?" Hodge asked.

"No. However, if your friend mistrusts you or hurts you in some way, it tears you apart. The reason is you have feelings for them. You trust them. They're the only ones that can truly cause hurt in your life. Do you understand

83

that?"

"Yeah, I see your point, but what does that have to do with it?" Hodge said.

"Hodge, when you left me, it hurt. I thought you were my friend. I never thought you'd abandon me. I was alone and scared. The pain I felt...I thought I'd lost you, or you were killed. It was devastating to me."

A blank look came over Hodge's face and after a long pause, he said, "Bob, you're my friend. I was scared too. I thought I'd lost you, that my friend had met the Devil. You were possessed."

"Maybe I was. Couldn't you talk to me?"

"There wasn't no talking to you! You were straight crazy with bloodlust, not the mission."

"Maybe you're right. Tomorrow is a new day. I've changed, too. I'll only take out targets that you agree on. If you don't want to, we won't. I'm sorry. A feeling came over me you couldn't possibly understand. Hodge, I wanna know where you went. If you don't want to tell me you don't have to."

"I went back here to get some supplies and think. I figured you would make it back here sooner or later. I knew you were getting low. I wanted to be alone and think things through, that's all. I didn't think about you getting lost or the GPS unit. You're a great tracker and navigator. The thought never crossed my mind. I could've gotten you killed. I'm sorry."

"It's over," I said.

"I'm ready to finish this mission and go home. Walk out proud for what we've accomplished."

"That's the Hodge I know. Let's get a plan in order. And remember my leg...nothing too far."

We sat down and pored over the map, trying to find a place that would offer both concealment and shooting opportunity. We agreed on what looked to be a great place about eight miles up the road. We found it on the other side, a location known as a hot spot for drug-trafficking and gun-running. We rolled up for a good night's sleep. We would make our way tomorrow the best that we could, and set up camp for the following day. We figured with my ankle it would take all day to travel the eight miles. It was settled. Tomorrow we were off on another big adventure. I was going to take it easy and be a good sniper.

The next morning we woke up and Hodge made a comment that was unlike him. "Bob, let's go. I've got some work to do."

"What did you say?" The word "work" registered in my mind as "killing."

"You heard me, let's go get this over with, go home, and forget about it."

"Are you really ready to do this? Are you going to shoot?"

"Not only am I going to do it, I'm taking the first shot and maybe the last."

"What the hell got into you?"

"Nothing, just ready to do my job, and that's how I see it from now on. It's not killing for pleasure or against the law. It's my job. My country wants me to do this, so I am going to do what has been asked of me."

"Holy shit! That's what I am talking about! Just don't shoot me."

We packed up for our last and final encounter, and off we went. The first mile or so, my ankle was killing me. We had to stop several times and give it a rest. After that, it seemed to loosen up and we were able to move a little faster. I still didn't think that we'd reach our position anytime soon, maybe by around 1600 hours or so. That would give us just enough time to settle in and wait. There was a possibility we might get in some night shooting. That would be fun, although, unfortunately, our targets would be able to see the muzzle blast and our position would be compromised. With my broken ankle, I would be a liability in our escape if someone came after us. I realized we had to be really careful in what we did, or we were in big trouble.

At about 1630 we arrived on the side of the mountain overlooking the road. Our position was about 650 yards away — a nice, easy shot. We both agreed that this was the place. After donning our ghillies, we made camp, figuring nothing was going to happen this late. We would be up bright and early in the morning to watch the road.

"Hodge, I think we need to cut down some of this brush, what do you think?"

"Yeah, give me the clippers, Crip. Just sit on your ass, look through your scope and tell me what to cut."

"This is the life. I've got my own slave now. I should've broken my ankle a long time ago."

"Shut up or I'll put a tourniquet on it."

"Just clip and hurry up."

It wasn't more than an hour after we'd gotten set up that I saw someone on a motorcycle. *What the hell is this about?* I thought. We watched him come to the border road from El Salvador, and then head back south.

"Hodge, what do you think of that?"

"Something's coming. We'd better be ready."

"What are you thinking?"

"Whatever comes out is definitely up to no good. We know this road is frequently used by the drug traffickers."

"Okay, so, was that someone scoping out the road?"

"I'll buy that."

"So, just start shooting when they come back?"

"Yeah. Open up on them."

"All right. Let's do it."

Within 20 minutes, the motorcycle returned. I could see him talking on the radio.

"That one's mine, Finger. You take whatever comes next."

"Okay."

Within minutes, a station wagon pulled in. Hodge

immediately shot the man off the bike. I was totally amazed at what was happening. I opened up on the wagon, where I thought the driver would be sitting. As the windshield started to shatter, the wagon lost control. It ran over the now dead motorcycle rider that Hodge shot and careened into the ditch. Silence. No activity, only the sound of the running wagon's engine. I didn't know if I gotten the driver. No one had bothered to try and come out the door. I figured the driver was dead and his foot had jammed the gas pedal, running over the dead cyclist in the process. After a moment of relief, another car sped through the barrier that we'd made, trying to access the road across the intersection. Hodge and I started shooting. We blew out a tire, but the car kept coming across the road, driving on a flat.

"Hodge, we can go around and cut him off if we move fast enough! There is no way he is gonna go that far! What do you think?"

"Let's go!"

We made our way around the mountain, looking for the road. Sure enough, there it was and dust was flying as the crippled car attempted its escape. I told Hodge to try and catch up with him. I'd never make with my bad ankle, but I had a good vantage point over the road and could keep long-range sniping in play. I wished Hodge luck, told him come back when it was over, and he took off running through the jungle. I tried to make my way up the mountain in order to get a shot at the car if it stopped. I kept my eye on Hodge as he made his way through the jungle. Then I noticed the trail of dust had stopped. The driver had stopped to fix the flat, just like we figured. I couldn't make out the driver, but could see the front of the car clear enough. A back tire was flat. The car was about 1,200 yards out — a little too far to make a shot on the front tires. Besides, if I missed, the driver would surely light out. I sat waiting for Hodge to make his grand entrance. He would be there in less than 15 minutes.

The sound of automatic weapons broke the silence in

the air. ***What the hell?*** The driver was obviously shooting at Hodge! He must have heard him coming through the underbrush. I tried to find the man in my scope. No luck. I did what I thought was the next best thing. I ranged myself to the tire and took a shot. If I hit the tire and the shooter came into view, I could take him out. Failing that, I hoped to make him stop shooting at Hodge. ***Why isn't Hodge taking a shot? Maybe he can't see the guy. What is going on?*** I heard the automatic weapon start again. I saw the shooter looking over his hood in Hodge's direction. I settled the crosshairs and waited for him to look up to begin shooting again. I decided to take out his driver's side window, hoping to draw him out. I squeezed off the shot, but hit nothing but dirt. ***Too low!*** The shooter broke and made a run for the other side of the road. I fired. The man was knocked forward several feet. It looked like he was hit by a car. ***What the hell? I need to know if Hodge is okay!*** I was about to move when I saw Hodge come out of the jungle and place several shots into the downed man, then start his way back to me. ***What's that about? The guy's gotta be dead!*** I realized that my shot hadn't found its mark, and Hodge had shot him at close range.

It struck me wrong. Why did Hodge shoot that man so many times? Was Hodge mad at him for shooting? Was he losing control? What would cause a man that had such a thrill for life to go off the deep end? Hodge hadn't been right since his disappearance. I wondered if he had flipped a little. I'd heard stories of it happening to men in wartime. Whatever had happened, I needed to talk to Hodge and get his version of the story. There was no reason to shoot a dead man five or six times in the back.

I sat on the mountain for what seemed an eternity, waiting for Hodge to make his way back. Eventually, Hodge came walking up like it was just another day in the sun.

"Hodge, what happened?"

"What do you mean?"

"Did he hear you come through the trees? Is that why he started shooting at you?"

"No, I told him I was coming."

"What!"

"I got up there and said 'Hey! Come out!' And he started shooting at me."

"What were you thinking, calling him out? He probably didn't even speak English!"

"I know."

"Hodge, what the hell! I wanna know what's going on."

"Nothing. I just needed to get a shot at him."

"I shot at the window trying to get him to move. He ran and I shot him in the back."

"Yeah, I shot him in the back too."

"Well, that explains why he flew forward so far. What was the deal with shooting him with the pistol several times?"

"You know, I can't really explain that. I just kept pulling the trigger. I guess I was just as surprised. Anyway, let's stay up here and see what happens tomorrow."

"Hodge, what are you talking about? We don't want to be here."

"They won't come looking for us. Besides, your ankle is messed up. Let's not travel. Let's watch."

"I don't think that's a good idea."

"Well, you ran the show the first half, now it's my turn."

"Okay."

We sat for about an hour. Another car approached from the west and stopped at the scene. We watched through our scopes as a lone figure walked around the mess. After taking a good look, the man started robbing the bodies. We sat there, watching him drag the bodies out and rifle through their pockets. When he'd finished, he started searching the vehicle, going through everything. We watched as the pillager continued his work. He'd been in the back seat for a long time, maybe five to 10 minutes, when he came out with a plastic bag about a foot square. He didn't make it to his car before Hodge split the top of his head with a silver jacket bullet. Then I heard him fire again.

"Hodge, what are you doing?"

"He's just as guilty as the others. Screw him, too."

"Why the hell are you shooting him twice?"

"Why not make sure he is dead?"

"Christ! You took off the top of his head! I think he's dead enough."

"What's wrong with you? Do your damn job!"

"Something's not right. Why are you shooting dead men?"

"I just feel like it. Now let's get ready for bed."

"No, I want to talk about all of this shit! I think there is something wrong with you. Have you flipped?"

"Nope. Just doin' my job."

We bedded down for the night with not more than a few words said. Something was definitely wrong. Why was Hodge doing this? Was it to teach me a lesson in control, or had he really just flipped? I didn't know the answer. One thing, however, was clear; Hodge bothered me. I really thought he's just lost it. He seemed so cold. Nothing seemed to bother him anymore. I personally wanted to head back to the DZ and wait for the next week. Hodge had gone crazy and now I was the sane one. *Funny how things start out one way and end another.*

I awoke in the middle of the night to the sound of crying. I heard Hodge weeping in his bag. Quietly, Hodge was praying — asking forgiveness and weeping uncontrollably. I didn't know what to do. I was glad to see Hodge was getting back to reality. *Now what do I do? Do I ask him what's wrong? Do I just go back to sleep?* I heard the sound of a button unbutton. That could only be one thing — *his pistol.* I rolled over.

"Hodge, what's going on? Tell me, buddy. Let's talk."

"I don't want to live any more, Bob."

"Why?"

"Something's wrong with me! I've never felt like this before!"

"Please tell me, Hodge."

"I have this awful feeling. I just want to start killing everyone! It's starting to become fun! I don't know why I feel like this, but it's scaring me. I can't get the men out of my mind. Just kill and kill. That's all I think about now. It's wrong, Bob! Something's not right with me. With you, maybe that'll be normal, but that's not me and you know it."

"Maybe this *is* you and you're just becoming aware of it yourself. And thanks a lot! Normal for me? Listen, I don't want you to do anything stupid like kill yourself."

"I'm not going to do that."

"Then why the pistol?"

"I don't know."

"Look, just talk. Tell me anything you want. I'll just listen."

"What do you want me to say? That I'm some psychotic killer now?"

"No, you're not. You're doing your job and that's all. You should be proud of what you are doing. I admire you so much. You're kind and giving. You have a great family. Look at you! You've made so much of your life already. Don't you think your grandfather ever felt like this?"

"I don't know."

"He probably did, but he did it for the country that he loved. He did what was asked of him, and so did so many others. Look at all those who died for this country. It wasn't for nothing. This is for our heritage, our way of life, for your family and mine. Remember, we didn't come down here on our own. We were asked, by our country, for help."

"I see your point, but I still have a hard time dealing

with it."

"Maybe you do, but look at all the people you're helping. You're doing what they can't. You are putting your life in danger for America. I don't mean the politicians. I mean the country. What it stands for. You're a secret hero. You'll always be one. Someday I'll write a book and make you famous. Clint Eastwood will play your part."

"Oh? And who would play your part, Charles Manson?"

"Damn it! Am I really that bad?"

"No, it's just since I've known you, you've been crazy. Nothing bothers you. You never get excited. You're always in control, but still psychotic. Everything you do is like another day. I don't think you have feelings for anything."

"That's not true. When you were gone, I missed you and I was scared of dying. Not really scared of dying; just being alone. I didn't like being out here by myself. You're my friend and I need you. Someday we'll laugh about all of this, and you know what? There will be others, like us, doing this exact same thing for our benefit and for our country. They'll go through the same struggles as you and I. Hopefully, they'll make it out and will go on with life. Life is full of struggles and challenges. Hodge, this is just a stepping stone. You made it. Let's finish the week and go home. If you want to go to the pick-up site and wait, I will go with you."

"No. Let's pick a new course and if something happens, it's God's will."

"Come here Hodge. Give me a hug. I love you, buddy. And if you ever tell anyone, I'll kill you."

We both laughed and hugged each other, then went back to sleep.

The next morning had an eerie feeling in the air.

"Hodge, are you awake?"

"Yeah."

"Something ain't right. Almost like we are not alone."

"Shit, Bob, look down there."

As I looked through my scope, I could see 30 or more Army personnel moving in our direction. There were people all around the car and motorcycle checking things out.

"Hodge, we gotta move out!"

We gathered up all our stuff, put on our ghillies, and started to move north.

"Hodge, stop! Someone's moving in from the other side of the mountain. I can hear 'em."

"Shit! Move slow and come with me."

We started moving east. It was the only direction with no one coming toward us. As we moved as silently as possible, I could hear my heart pounding. The anxiety of being caught was suffocating. From here on out, Hodge and I used only hand signals to communicate.

As we made our way down the mountain, I could hear men talking and moving up behind us. Their pace was faster than ours. We were trying to move in stealth — they were walking at normal pace and talking. I could feel them getting closer. The idea of stopping and trying to make a stand was becoming prominent in my thoughts. We had to keep going. There had to be 50-60 of them coming from everywhere. My ankle was killing me, and I knew I couldn't outrun anyone. I would have to stand and fight. I was putting Hodge's life in danger now.

We had just made it to the bottom when Hodge and I found ourselves looking straight at a guy standing not more than 20 feet from us, smoking a cigarette. We slowly dropped to the ground, trying not to make a sound. The man just stood there beside a log, looking up the mountain, apparently acting as a sentry. We so close we couldn't even breathe without being heard. How he hadn't heard us coming down the mountain was a mystery. I took out my knife and inched toward a nearby log. If he walked by I could kill him silently, so no warning could be made.

I gave Hodge the indication of what I was about to do. He nodded his approval. I saw Hodge take out his pistol for backup. I slowly slithered up to a dead piece of wood not far from where I was. I tried to blend in as much as possible and make no sound. If the sentry gave a warning, we were dead. All those men against two of us? It would turn into a battle for sure, but I didn't want that. *Why is this guy standing by himself smoking? What's he doing so far from the road?* There were only two plausible answers: He was a sentry watching this side of the mountain for us, or he was looking clues as to who'd been here. The only flaw in that logic was he wasn't moving or looking for anything. He just stood or sat, looking at the mountain. He had no radio or arms with the exception of an old, rusted pistol.

Ten minutes went by and nothing happened. I could see and hear the men on the mountain. They'd found our campsite. There was quite a commotion up there. My heart had never pounded so hard. I wanted to kill this guy and start shooting, just to kill the suspense. *Please move. I have to get out.* I could see many of the men up on the mountain inspecting our campsite. *Damn it! We should have left it more concealed! Cleaned it up better!* We'd been in too much of hurry to get out of there. I started thinking about Hodge. I was kind of mad at him. He was the one that wanted to stay, not me. I knew better. What were his intentions in staying? Getting caught and paying for his crimes, wanting to die or kill more people? I didn't know. My instincts had told me to move on last night. I should have, but Hodge had made me feel guilty.

The sentry got up and started walking in my direction. He stopped five feet from me, still looking up the mountain. How did he not hear my heart beating? Then he stepped right in front of me, and turned his back. It was as if he knew I was there and he wanted to die. How had he never

94

seen Hodge or me? As I lay there, I started praying for this man leave the area and let us be on our way. I really didn't want to kill him. I thought he might be Honduran and didn't want to make a mistake and accidentally kill the wrong guy. I just kept thinking, *They're not supposed to be in the area.*

With the great news of finding our spot on the hill, the sentry started walking in the direction from which we had come. We sat there for a little while, allowing him to get out of earshot, then I motioned to Hodge. We made our way back up the other mountain and all the dead fall trying to get back to the drop zone. *The jig is up. They're onto us. We need to move out of this country.* It was obvious they knew we were there. Looking back on it, we'd moved all over, but were never in the same place twice. It wouldn't take a genius to figure out that someone might be waiting at the next crossroads. Who were these men? I assumed they were not Hondurans. The Hondurans were supposed to know we were there. Why would the El Salvadorians, and military no less, be across the border looking for us? Something was wrong. The only way to get any answers was to talk to American Intelligence.

As we started to approach the top of the next mountain, we slowed to take a look behind us. We sat there, caught our breath, and gave my ankle a rest. We could see personnel walking all over the mountain. It appeared we'd been compromised. What we saw was something else. We could see at least 30 to 40 men on just that one side of the mountain. They looked like ants on an anthill. I told Hodge we needed to get as far away as possible. We had to get back to the pick-up zone and away from El Salvador.

Slowly, we started back to the drop zone. We needed more supplies and rest. We had had too close a call and that was it. Our intention was get back undetected, hang around the DZ and wait for pick-up. As we traveled, me hobbling, we encountered more men in front of us. The strangest part was these were Army personnel. *What the hell is going on?*

Had someone told them where we were and let them have us? I started to feel we were part of a government experiment. It may sound strange, but I had heard of these types of operations being run. Sending us in, tell the other government where we are, but only send in 40 personnel. We'll see who gets whom. It sounded far-fetched, but how else could these people know where we were every minute, and where we were going? It was like they had a copy of our map with the points of interest laid out.

"Hodge, you think these guys were tipped off? Maybe someone told them where we are."

"Why would anybody do that?"

"I don't know. Maybe somebody's running some op to see if 40 Honduran army men can catch us, make us talk, or worse, kill us."

"Why would our government do that?"

"How can you explain all these Army personnel everywhere? They know we are right here somewhere and they're trying to find us. These aren't El Salvadorians, they're too far north. They're Hondurans. Something's wrong."

"I hope you're wrong, but it does sound like there might be some truth to it."

"Think about it. We want to prove that our elite force is better than any other country. How better to prove it? We'll send two of our guys into your country and you send, say, no more than 40 personnel to find them. It's like a game of chess. Who's better — two Americans or 40 Hondurans? And you know it'll all be covered up. Black Ops is famous for covering things up. Never let the public know what's going on. Just like us being here. Remember in the meeting? 'You are not down there. This is a top-secret mission.' All deniable. What kinda shit is that? Hodge, we've been set up!"

"Quit it! You're freaking me out."

"Well, how else can you explain this? They give us

96

three weeks to get to know the country and then turn the dogs loose on us."

"Bob, let's get home and back to the zone."

"All right, but just think about it. Hodge, we need to change course. Go back to northwest. We gotta try and avoid these personnel. I'm thinking that our drop zone is compromised, too."

"No. You're being paranoid."

"Well, something is wrong. We never saw anyone this far before, especially military personnel."

"Let's move to the drop zone. We'll keep our eyes and ears open."

"I'll bet that it's been found, and if it has, we've been sold out."

"Shut up, Bob! Our government wouldn't do that."

"Why not? We're expendable. I'm telling you, if I hear any shit about accidents to the others that came over here, I am telling somebody. If the government's going pull this, screw 'em!"

"They didn't do this. If that's true, then they should know we're here, right?"

"Yeah."

"Well, they obviously don't know."

"Yeah, that is weird. Hodge, we gotta to be really careful. If we shoot, we'll give away our position. We need to be stealthy. Move around slow until pick-up time. I'm thinking we don't even go back to the drop zone. Screw it. Let's move away and keep circling until its time."

"Yeah, I think you might be right. If the government did this crap, somebody's gonna to pay."

"You got that right."

We made a wide circle around the personnel we'd spotted, trying to come into the DZ from the north. Every direction we looked, we could see people moving. The feeling was definitely eerie.

"Hodge, look right there — fresh tracks. Someone's

been here this morning."

"Looks like more than one, too," Hodge added.

"Something's wrong. You don't think we killed Hondurans instead of El Salvadorians, do you? Maybe that's why they are after us. Could we have messed up?"

"Please quit it! I can't take much more of this."

"Fine. Let's keep traveling."

We were about five miles from our DZ. Something wasn't right. The whole place was crawling with military personnel. We were slowly making our way down a gulch, and crossing over a stream when Hodge slipped and fell down the mud-slick mountain and landed in a murky pond. From my position, I couldn't see what the hell he had fallen into. I slowly made my way down the embankment and saw Hodge, holding his rifle over his head, trying to make it to the other side. I started making my way around the hill to the other side. I guessed that Hodge fallen about 20 feet into the pond, but he appeared to be all right.

I finally made it to the other side and Hodge. He was not a happy camper. He just looked up at me from the water and said, "Fuck this place."

"I can't agree more, Hodge, but at least you're okay. Let's get the hell out of here. I think everyone heard you fall down the mountain."

"Fuck them! Let 'em come! I'm ready to fight these stupid bastards!"

"Settle down."

"No! Let's just kill them! Why are we running anyway? We can take 'em all and you know it!"

"Maybe we can, but they have an limitless supply of men and there's only two of us. Besides, our government obviously isn't going to help us. We're on our own, unless you're ready to die."

"What do you mean?"

"We take on that army, we'll die and you know it. We can kill a shit load, but they'd get us eventually. Will our government ever acknowledge us being down here if this blows up into some kinda scandal? Not a chance."

Hodge got out of the pool and haphazardly dried himself off. I chuckled as I watched him brush off the muck. We started back on our general line of direction prior to Hodge's fall, and continued moving slowly through jungle. Once again, we found a lookout. We stopped, waited, and prayed for darkness to fall. My curiosity was starting to get the better of me. *If by morning they haven't found us, will they send more personnel to cover more ground?* I thought we should consider moving past our DZ, in case it was being watched. I thought we should head north a few miles for a day or two and let things die down.

"Hodge, what do you think? Keep going or go to DZ?"

"We have enough food."

"I say we keep going for a few days. We can come closer in when the pick-up time arrives."

"Yeah, that's a good idea. The farther we get away, the better."

"Give me a grid with the GPS. Let's find out exactly where we are."

"Here, 5555, 5555. That puts us about two miles from the DZ."

"You wanna take a peek from a distance? See if they found it?"

"Sure, but let's not get too close. I think you're right. They're watching it and are waiting for us to return."

We made it up a little ravine and found a lookout sitting about 100 yards from us. Two other men appeared to be looking at our camp. Now I started worrying more than usual. It was apparent now that they were looking for us — and they had no idea that we were already there.

The pieces started coming together. Our government had lied to us! We'd been set up for a training exercise.

"Hodge, what do you think?"

"Let's move back down the mountain, loop around, and try to head north like you said."

"All right. Follow me."

We slowly made our way back down the ravine and looped our way around the mid-base of the hill toward the north. We both knew that there could be people everywhere now. We had to be extremely cautious, take it easy from here on out, and move in stealth.

We made our way past the DZ and came upon a road.

"Hodge, what you wanna do? Wait 'til dark or try and make it?"

"Let's wait. Just watch the road and wait until dark. With you gimped up and the road right here, they'd get us in no time."

"Okay. We'll hang out and wait until dark. Then we'll get across and make our way north."

Night came. We put on our night vision goggles and were watching up and down the road, until we picked a curved section of the road to cross. This allowed a vantage point from only one direction. We finally decided the area was clear and we crossed the road with ease. After crossing, we started north, heading closer to our main pick-up site. I detected the odor of a cigarette.

"Hodge, can you smell that?"

"Yeah. Smells like a cigarette."

You can actually smell a cigarette for several hundred yards.

"Hodge, can you see anything?"

"No."

"Keep moving north."

We started using our lensatic compasses to move through the night. My ankle was killing me with every step. I needed to take off my boot and let my ankle get some circulation, but under the circumstances, I couldn't risk taking the chance of getting caught. We needed to move on, so we kept moving straight north. I figured we would move at least five miles north and that would put us within six miles of our main pick-up site.

At around 2000 hours my ankle couldn't take much more.

"Hodge, I need to rest. Take my boot off."

"Yeah, I haven't seen a sign of anyone for a while."

I took off my boot only to find my ankle black, blue, yellow, and very, very swollen.

"Jesus, look at that!"

"Man, Bob, I think you broke something!"

"I don't know. But I know one thing, I can't keep walking on this much longer. I need to rest for a few hours. Get some blood circulating to my ankle. Besides, we need a catnap."

"Okay. Take a nap and I'll stand guard."

"Thanks."

Hodge shook my shoulder, rousing me from my nap.

"What's wrong?"

"Get your boot on."

I put my boot and checked my watch. It was 2420.

"What are we gonna do? You hear something?"

"Bob, put your boot on and follow me. I'll explain later."

I finished putting on the boot, pulled on my pack, and started following Hodge. He moved very slowly in a northern direction. *What the hell is going on?* I waited, then moved on. I figured Hodge would let me know soon enough. Suddenly, I heard what sounded like a helicopter. *Is that what Hodge heard?*

"Hodge, what's up?"

"Something is going on over the hill. I saw one helicopter fly over while you were sleeping. We need to see if it's theirs or ours."

At least now I knew what had prompted our move.

"Hodge, that's a Huey. That's one of ours. What in Christ's sake is it doing here? We still have five days before

101

the pick-up."

"I don't know, but let's go."

"Sounds good to me."

We made our way up the hill. My ankle was about to explode. I could hardly walk. Thank God for adrenaline. Getting the hell out of there was much more important than the pain. We finally climbed to the top of a little knoll. There was quite commotion down below. The helicopter had landed and personnel were moving all over the area.

"Hodge, what do you think?"

"Looks like some kind of party, but we ain't invited."

I looked through my scope. The best I could come up with, the Huey was one of ours, but there were no markings on the side. It might be either.

"Hodge, can you tell anything?"

"Looks like one of ours, but I ain't sure."

"Can you tell what's going on? Look at that in the chopper. It's boxes of some kind."

"Yeah, but what the hell's in 'em?"

"One thing for sure, we need to stay right here."

"Amen to that."

We were about 1,100 yards from the site of the entertainment. Hodge and I stayed put for about an hour, observing and taking down notes. Hodge took some pictures in hopes they would turn out. The moon was full moon, so there was a good chance that some of them would be usable. Then, the military would have some explaining to do. We continued to do what recon snipers do the best — we sat there, took notes and observed. The main activity was an exchange of boxes. There were people everywhere, and as far as we could tell, no Americans. The chopper finally took off and flew overhead. Hodge took several pictures of it. After the chopper left, the personnel split up and appeared to be leaving.

"Hodge, we need to get the hell out of here. Even farther than before. Something's wrong. We're in the wrong place at the wrong time."

"Let's move."

We made tracks heading directly north. It was about 0400 when I asked Hodge to stop. My ankle couldn't take any more. I sat down and took off my boot, and found my ankle completely swollen. I couldn't believe my luck. My ankle was either badly sprained or maybe broken. It hurt, but my only thought was to get the hell out of there.

"Hodge, I need to lie down and keep my leg elevated. I will stay awake and you try and get some sleep."

"All right."

Hodge drifted off to sleep. I looked up at the stars and wondered what was actually happening. Thoughts of betrayal and mistrust flowed through my head like the wind in the trees. *If the government has actually sent us down here for an exercise, will we ever find out, or will they just deny it? If they haven't, how could these military personnel be all over us? Why aren't they on the other side looking for El Salvadorians? They must know we are here. What the hell was that helicopter doing here? Was it American, or did it just look like one of ours? There are lots of Huey helicopters out there. What does this all mean?* I assured myself that my questions would never be answered.

My thoughts were interrupted by weeping. I looked over to find my only friend crying in his sleep. Poor Hodge was such a good guy. He was losing it. I promised myself when we got back I would take him to a minister or a priest to give him some counseling. He was an emotional wreck. This whole experience had been devastating to him. On the other hand, I wouldn't have changed a thing. What a rush it'd been. It takes a certain type of individual to do what we do, and Hodge wasn't one of them. In order to be in special ops, you needed not only the physical capability, but the mindset as well. You're told up front you'll be asked to do things for your country that others won't. The regular Marines are only asked during wartime, not during peacetime. That's the difference.

Hodge finally got up.

"What time is it, Bob?"

"Its 0800. Time to head out."

I put on my boot and stood up.

"Hodge, let's try and make it about a mile or less from the pick-up site today."

"Sounds good. Boy, I needed that rest. I feel a lot better."

"Give me a grid and let's see how far we gotta go."

Hodge spurted out the grid and, surprisingly, we were within two miles of our pick-up site.

"Well, ol' man, let's head out and keep our eyes open," Hodge said.

We started heading down a little slope when Hodge stopped me.

"Bob, tell my family, if I don't make it, that I love them."

It caught me totally off guard.

"What are you talking about? If you die, so will I."

"You have the gift of life."

"What do you mean?"

"Finger, you can't die. Look at how many times you should have been dead, and nothin'."

"Like when?"

"Remember the cliff in Bridgeport, California? You fell over the side and only knocked yourself out. That had to be a 100 feet or so. Most people would've died. Remember when your chute didn't open and you pulled your spare? The only reason you're alive is the trees caught your canopy. Once again, what happened to you? You were knocked out. Bob, you have a gift for living. The only reason that I can imagine is you don't care about life."

"I care about life. I don't wanna to die."

"What's your favorite saying?" Hodge asked.

"What?"

"'Another day in Hell.'"

"I'm just kidding," I protested.

"What about when someone asks you how you are doing? Your response is always the same: 'Praying for a heart attack.'"

"Yeah, but that's just me. It's not that I mean it. I just say that."

"Face it, you will live forever because you don't care about life. The people that care about and love life, die."

"Look, I am tired of discussing this crap. If we get compromised, I am the one that's hobbled, not you. If we get attacked, you get the hell out of here. I'll hold them off as long as I can. You need to think positive. We're gonna to make it out of this shit hole, both alive and kicking. Then we are going to find some answers. Who loves you?"

"You do, jackass."

"Now, let's get the hell out of here and find a whore with VD for me. I'm starting to think the clap would be better than this place."

We both laughed.

We made it within 500 yard from the pick-up site. Looking through our scopes, the sight we saw disturbed us. It appeared someone had been there. We decided we should circle, look for tracks or anything out of the ordinary, and come together on the other side. We started out. I went left and Hodge went right.

It wasn't to long before I found candy wrappers. I found two sets of tracks in the mud. Both pair of feet were small, say sizes six and seven. *Really small for men — for Americans, anyway.* These could be the tracks of Hispanics. Their feet are generally smaller. I looked at where the tracks led and they appeared headed right to our landing site. *What do I do now? Follow the tracks or meet up with Hodge?* I continued to head in the direction toward Hodge. We could come back together and follow the tracks. Within 10 feet of the first tracks and I ran into another set. This time the footprints were very far apart. This could only mean one thing — this individual was carrying something heavy. A man caring a heavy load spreads his feet apart wider and makes a shorter step in order to keep his center of gravity. This individual was carrying a load, and whoever made the first set of tracks wasn't. *What the hell is he carrying? Why aren't the other two carrying anything?* I started moving again. I found a canteen that one of them had dropped. *This isn't making any sense.* I started heading toward Hodge. I was curious as to what he'd found. When I finally meet up with him, he was holding a 30-round magazine full of 7.62 rounds.

"Hodge, what'd you find?"

"Couple of sets of prints. Moving east to west and north and south."

"What?"

"Yeah, they're goin' all over the place. Looks like they're setting up lookouts in every direction."

I told him what I'd found, and suggested we move to the alternate pick-up site. I believed this one had been compromised. We needed to get the hell out of that place.

"I don't know about you Hodge, but I don't feel comfortable sitting here for four days."

"No, let's go to the alternate — but, you know what that means?"

"Two extra days."

"We could sit up high, stay around here and observe. See if they come back."

"Yeah. Let's do that. If they start to come back, then we'll know someone gave us away and we'll move to the alternate."

Hodge and I moved about a mile from the pick-up site. We set up on the top the most remote hill close by. We set up camp and I took off my boot. We took turns for the next couple of days watching for personnel. We saw nothing, but we did notice more helicopters fly by during the night.

Why were they coming now? It was very interesting. The whole time we had been there — nothing. And *now* military and helicopters coming from everywhere? Something didn't add up.

When pick-up day arrived, everything seemed normal. We were finally going to get out of this hellhole. Pick-up was at 2300 hours and the clock was ticking.

"We're going home, Hodge."

"The chopper ain't here yet and it's ain't 2300 hours."

"Will you shut up? Just once say 'yes, we're going home, this is great' and bullshit me a little."

"All right. Everything's goin' great. Let's get ready to go and catch our flight home. Is that better?"

"I feel so much better."

Hodge and I sat upon the mountain for the rest of the day. The coast was clear. At 2000 hours we finally moved toward the pick-up site. Something still didn't seem right.

"Hodge, how do you feel?"

"Like I am going to be sick."

"Yeah, me too."

"Something ain't right, is it?"

"No, but maybe we just can't imagine goin' home and anxiety is kickin' in."

"You could be right."

We stayed around the pick-up zone about a 100 yards out, waiting on the chopper to make its appearance. Then those wonderful sounds of blades cutting through the wind came over the horizon. When the chopper lit up the skies, we made it down to the pick-up site. The chopper sat down and we moved in. This had to be the best feeling in the world, sitting with Americans looking back at us. Taking us back home...or so we thought.

Chapter 8
Interrogation

The chopper came and we were all picked up, I guess. I never saw any of the others that were put out on the post. The next few days were not something I care to go through ever again. We were flown for about two hours to a set up U.S. military camp. As soon as we arrived, we were separated and from that moment on, did not see each other for days afterwards. When we landed, a Marine Sergeant told us to follow him. We looked at each other, wondering why. I didn't have a good feeling about this, but what are you supposed to do? I felt like I was in trouble. Maybe it was just my guilty conscience playing tricks on me again.

The sergeant directed me into a room by myself. I was instructed put all my effects into a box that was stationed by the bed. He was very firm. Everything in my pack and clothes had to be placed in the box. Nothing was to be left out. I went into the room. He followed. I stripped everything off and placed it all into the box. Everything — spent ammo casings, pack, clothes, boots, socks, weapons...everything I owned — with the exception of my dog tags and ID card. The sergeant placed the box outside my door and told me to wait; he would be back.

I assumed that Hodge was going through the same scenario. I wasn't sure what all of this was about. I tried to stay patient. I sat naked in the room for about an hour. The sergeant came back in and instructed me to follow him to the showers. He threw me a towel, soap, razor, and toothbrush. I took a shower, cleaned up, and was escorted back to my room, all under surveillance of the sergeant. When got back to my room, a new set of clothes was on the chair. I was instructed to put them on, but not to leave the room. Breakfast would be delivered.

I spent the whole day in the room being waited on hand and foot. There was nothing to do but read magazines, use the restroom, and wonder what the hell was going on.

The next morning I was allowed to shower again. I started to question my guard.

"What's going on? Why am I being treated like a prisoner?"

"I was instructed not to talk to you or answer any questions."

He obviously didn't know any aspects of our mission or was privileged to any information. I accepted that, but the suspense was killing me. ***Was I in trouble or what?***

That afternoon, I was called to appear in front of the board. Not good! I sat in a chair facing four high ranking officers. The questions started coming.

"Are you being cared for properly? Do you need anything?"

"No, sir. Everything's fine."

"Tell us about your mission. Everything that happened."

I began my recount, starting with the personnel that Hodge and I assumed to be the targets of opportunity. They set their recording devices and took notes. I was nervous. I decided that I wouldn't lie. I would tell them everything. So I began. They continued to listen, periodically stopping me to ask questions.

When I'd finished the whole story, questions started to come back. They started at the beginning and, step-by-step, picked apart everything that I said and did. This didn't help my feelings of anxiety. I could see the officers looking at each other, passing notes, and looking at me. I was a nervous wreck.

At the end of the whole routine, they asked me what I felt about the situation.

"I was uncomfortable. I wasn't sure who the enemy was. What about the Hondurans? It seemed we were comprised."

Pin drop.

"Was this an exercise? Is the government trying to test our troops against theirs?" I continued.

This didn't go over so well. Their replies were not quite good enough to keep me from thinking of it further.

"We'll look into the matter and get back to you."

They never did.

At the end of a very long interrogation, I was instructed never to speak about the mission to anyone, not even my partner. I was sworn to secrecy. They reminded me that I would remain separated for the next few days and there would be another meeting.

So, for the next three days I sat it in my room without any contact with the outside. I had one reoccurring thought: Why'd they take all my things? I never got the chance to ask that question. Maybe at the next meeting I'd get the chance.

On the fourth day, a knock came at the door. I was led down the hall into another room with one individual and a machine. *Fuck me! A lie detector!* Talk about shitting yourself! *Oh, no! I'm in deep shit, now! They thought I was lying! Or they are going to make sure I didn't lie!*

A Major, manning the lie detector, sat me down in a chair, started strapping cords all around me, and finally strapped one onto my finger.

"Try and relax."

He'd just as soon told a damn steer to relax at a slaughterhouse. My heart must have been pumping extremely fast. He made mention several times to try and relax. *I must look guilty.* I kept running through everything in my mind. What had I left out? Did I fib on some of the issues? Stretch some? I was about to lose it.

Finally, the first questions came and that was easy. He told me to answer yes to the first two questions.

"Is your name…" he began, stating my name.

"Yes."

"Have you ever served in the U.S. Army?"

"Yes."

I hadn't. He was establishing a baseline for lies versus the truth.

"Did you lie to any of the board or their questions?"

"No."

"Did you shoot and kill anyone in the last month?"

"Yes."

"Did you shoot anyone that could have possibly not have been a target of opportunity?"

I tried to respond with an answer other than yes or no. No good.

"Answer the question, yes or no! Did you shoot anyone that was not a target of opportunity?"

"No."

In my mind, they were all guilty. The ones I shot, anyway. I was clear on that one.

"Did you follow all protocol with your duty as a sniper?"

"No."

I knew I was in trouble now. I did fire more than one shot. I gave my position away. I had left my partner. Hell, I did everything that I was trained not to do! So yes, I was guilty. I had already told the board that. The questions continued for about an hour. When I was done with the questions, I'll be damned if he didn't go back through the entire list again. I guess they try to confuse you. Turn you all around. He asked several questions that were the same, just in different context.

By the time I was done and out of there, I felt like I'd run a marathon. I was totally drenched in sweat. I was a nervous wreck. I had visions of going to Leavenworth for war crimes. It was the most stressful thing I'd ever gone through. I didn't know if I was going to jail or going home, but I knew one thing: I was a little nervous about what Hodge was going to say about me. I knew he wouldn't have too many good things to say. I could already hear him. I was some kind of psycho. He was scared for his life. Aaaaaaaaahhhhhhhhh! I wanted this to be over with!

Two more days passed. I was mentally drained and worn out. At this point, I was about dead. I had worried myself sick for days now. I didn't know what Hodge had said. Had they found out that I was lying about something? Was I guilty of war crimes? I couldn't take it anymore. They sent me out there! They're the ones who made me a psycho. Why should I be doing all the suffering? The worst part was, I didn't know if anyone else was going through the same thing. Was I singled out because of my psychotic behavior and problems with Hodge?

A wonderful knock came at the door. I was requested to go for more round questioning. This could only be compared with to a man on death row, walking down that hall to be put to death. That's how I felt. I reached the interrogation room and there sat the chair in front of the firing squad waiting to question the guilty again. As if once hadn't been enough!

They asked the same old questions. How I was doing? Is everything okay? This time, I let them have it.

"Am I some kind of criminal? I've had no outside communication. I can't speak to my buddies. I've got a guard outside my door and no one is telling me what this is about."

They just looked at me as though I'd lost my mind. They weren't far off. One high ranking officer looked at me and said, "I understand this has been a long, strenuous, and tiresome. It's about to be over. You've been trained for this type of situation. Stay calm and relax. This is no different than what a POW would go through in wartime. The main thing is to relax. Whatever happens…happens."

I guess he was talking about the psychological impact of being questioned and isolated. I must have I failed that part of the mission. The way I saw it, I was being

112

pronounced guilty by my own country, not some foreign nation.

"Do you feel guilty for anything that has transpired in the last month?"

The polygraph guy had asked me the same question.

"Yes."

"Explain your answer."

"My partner wasn't acting right. I might have pushed him over the edge. I blame myself for that. I wasn't always sure that I followed proper protocol with my training. You know, leaving my partner, firing more than one shot. Trying to kill them all instead of just eliminating the head of the outfit."

They passed some more notes around.

"How is your mental state, after taking another human life?"

"It doesn't really bother me. It was my job, not for pleasure. It was for the country. I was told these guys are the ones who would kill children in our country, how they needed to be stopped. I was following orders. Carry out the mission to the fullest. The same as I've done my whole military career."

After all was said and done, the one that sat in the middle asking most of the questions reminded me, "Everything that has happened is classified. Top Secret. Never to be talked about again, not to your partner, not to anyone."

"Yes, sir. I will never speak of it."

"Would you like to talk to a counselor about the situations that have transpired?"

"I don't need one. I just wanna go home and get back to my unit. Am I in some kind of trouble?"

"No. This is normal operating procedure for these kinds of missions. Although you didn't follow total protocol, you didn't appear to have lied or committed a misuse of authority. You have accomplished what was asked by your command."

That last statement made me melt inside. I *wasn't* in any kind of trouble! What a great relief!

"How do you feel about your partner? His mental state?"

"Maybe I pushed him into doing things he wasn't ready to do. I was too gung-ho and couldn't slow down. How's he doing with all this interrogation? He wasn't doing so well last time I saw him. I'm worried about him."

"Your partner described what happened in the field between the two of you. I will relay this to you, to ease your conscience. He told this panel, if it weren't for men like you in the field, he wouldn't have made it out. He told us you kept your wits, kept the situation in control at all times. You made him feel more secure about the mission. So, with that in mind, we, the board, thank you for your dedication to the country and to your fellow soldier."

The officer in the middle finally got up, came over to me and shook my hand. He told me that the sergeant at the door would now escort me to my new quarters. I would return to the group. I was escorted back to my room. I collected all my stuff and followed him to a 10-man tent.

As I went in, I noticed about five guys sitting inside. All of them were part of the same unit. My curiosity was killing me.

"Where's everyone else?"

"Probably still getting some in."

I figured my time there was over, but there was still no Hodge.

One of the guys spoke up. "You okay?"

He was a much older Marine and had obviously been through this process many times. I started to talk, but he stopped me in mid sentence.

"Don't mention anything about the mission. You go to the interrogator school?"

"I didn't even know such a school existed."

"After this, they'll send ya. It's helpful for people in our profession. They teach you how to interrogate and how to be interrogated."

"What's the school about? What happens there?"

He told me a little, but the rest, he said, "you'll have to find out on your own." Typical. All the tough schools we're put through, no one leaks any information. They want you to experience the same things they did. But he did give me some information.

"First thing you'll notice in an interrogation is the layout of the room. The physical layout is the most important. For one thing, it'll make you very nervous the first time you go in."

No surprise there. I could very easily recall it being that and more in my interrogation room.

"Usually, they'll make you very uncomfortable with some crappy chair sitting in the middle of a small room. They'll either have chairs or stand over the top of you. Makes you feel powerless. They use a recorder, taping device, and a video. Now the video is the more important of the two. They can go back through it and monitor your movements, body language, and eye gestures. The first thing they try to do is develop a rapport with you. Try and make you relaxed, even though you are not. They'll ask you simple questions."

I recalled being asking how I was doing. If everything was okay me. This all made sense.

"These simple questions establish a baseline for truth, so the questions they start out with don't require much thinkin'. Now, during this phase, they're watchin' your eye movements."

I didn't understand what he meant by that, but he was leading up to an answer.

"If you're recalling a memory of an actual event, your eyes will fall to the right, 'cause this goes to the creative thinkin' part of your brain. Your eyes fall to that side — the memory side. Now if your eyes move to the left, means you are trying to make somethin' up — indicates deception. Your eyes'll play tricks on ya, whether ya know it or not. So what they do is ask you a question and watch your eyes. That determines what part of the brain you're thinkin' with. It's also nice if they're videotaping ya. They can go back and replay the questions and look at the eye movement to see how you're processing the information."

This didn't help me. I wished I'd had known this piece of information a little sooner.

"One of the most important things you can do while being interviewed is never let your eyes move. Be very aware of what they're doing. Look at who's asking the questions. Never stop staring at their eyes. Total eye contact at all times. Leaves no chance for interpretation on their part." He continued, "Easiest way of giving yourself away is bein' nervous. Body language, sweatin', fidgetin' — just being uncomfortable. Never tap your leg or your foot. Keep your hands to your side or on your knees and keep constant eye contact. Remember all that and they'll have a hard time tellin' anything. Now, there is the lie detector. There's ways of beating that. Takes lots of training, but you'll get that in school. I'll give ya' a hint. They usually read the questions to ya first, before they ask. Gives ya time to think about the ones ya know ya don't wanna answer. Starts the process of makin' ya nervous. Course, during questioning, they'll ask ya the same question a number of times, just to make sure they got the correct response. Now what ya gotta do is not think about the question at all. Just answer and go back to thinkin' of somethin' else. What I mean is, get a mindset of an event, maybe a family function, and just start daydreamin' about that. Most of your conscience is consumed with that and the questions they are askin' ya are just a small part. If ya think about the questions too much, about what they're askin' ya, you'll fail. Keep that in mind and you should have an easier time in the school. Course, they'll teach you all kind of neat tricks. That's somethin' ya have to experience for yourself. Not having a conscience could be your best friend. Remember that."

He went on telling me more. Some I heard, some not. It was great. It took time away from just sitting there wondering about Hodge. As I looked at the other guys in the room, I didn't recognize any of them. They were from other units. They weren't from my area in Camp Pendleton. I just sat there and made idle chat. We spent some time walking around bullshittin' about nothing — what we were going to be doing when we got home, and so on. It made me feel good to hang out with them, especially since I appeared to be the youngest of the group and the least experienced. Most of them had been in the Marines eight years or more. They were all pretty salty. I hadn't been in that long. I just got lucky. My shooting skills, not experience, got me into the sniper program.

That night I was lying in my bunk when Hodge arrived. He came strolling in, but looked like he'd been through Hell. He saw me. We hugged each other and said we were glad that was over with. Hodge lay in the bunk next to me. We started talking about what we were going to do as soon as we got back. Of course, the prostitute came up. I told him I would take the cheaper one. We laughed like old times.

The next week we spent most of the time sitting around playing Spades. We had a lot of fun, not talking one bit about the mission. But I really needed to talk about it. I was going to wait until Hodge and I got home to discuss it. I wanted to see if he'd gone through what I had. We just sat around, walked around, and made idle conversation. After about a week, we were called up to main office. There were 10 of us standing in a formation when a full bird Colonel walked out and gave us a little speech.

"As Marines, you have performed an exemplary mission. You have accomplished the objectives set forth for you. You men are what the Marines are about. This is how we show the world we are a force to be reckoned with. We sent out 10 Marines. Ten Marines came home. You should all be very proud of what you have accomplished. For that the Marine Corps is grateful. Very few Marines get the opportunity that you 10 have had. You have helped a foreign country, and in return, you have helped your country. This is training that only those in wartime receive. Some will never receive it. You were asked to perform a duty that not only went against some of your morals, but also will deeply affect some of you the rest of your lives. You performed this task because of your dedication to duty and you performed to Marine Corps standards. I am proud to offer you each this medal for your bravery and dedication."

We each were given a medal for a job well done. It was a great medal. I was very proud of it. We all just sat there and glowed. When the Colonel was done, he gave us a proper salute and dismissed us. Our plane was on the runway. We were going home.

Hodge and I walked back to the tent to gather our things and headed to the plane. I looked over to him.

"Is my medal bigger than yours?" They were both the same, but I just wanted to be funny.

"I really didn't deserve this."

That really bothered me. He did deserve it. He was still having a hard time dealing with everything. I grabbed him by the shoulder. "Hodge, did Grandpa get one of those?"

He looked at me and smiled.

"Grandpa's looking down sayin', 'That's my boy.'"

I think that boosted his spirits.

We boarded the C-5, strapped ourselves in and the plane made its way down the runway. The front end picked up and we were gliding. I looked over at Hodge.

"Hope we don't crash."

He looked at me like he wanted to throw me out. I just laughed and nudged him in the ribs. My friend and I were going home.

When we landed I looked at Hodge. "Well, we're home."

"Yeah, we'll never have to do that again. We only have two years left and I'm getting out."

But it wasn't over for either one of us. We just didn't know it yet.

Chapter 9
1ˢᵀ Sergeant Press – the Story of a Marine

Not long after we had been deployed to Desert Storm, I was walking back to my foxhole when I heard someone mumbling in the back of a Hum-V. Our Hummers had vinyl tops, making it impossible to see who was inside. So I did what anyone would have done; I opened the back flap. Inside I found a most frightening sight — 1ˢᵗ Sergeant Press.

1ˢᵗ Sergeant Press was an unimpressive 150 lbs. and quite possibly the meanest person I'd ever met. He hated everyone and everyone hated him. He was a Marine lifer, had spent five years in Vietnam, and by all accounts, was a raging alcoholic. But as with any life, there is always a story. I was about to find out the reason behind his meanness and madness.

1ˢᵗ Sergeant Press had been awarded the Navel Cross and five Silver Stars. He had so many medals and ribbons on his chest it made most men stand in awe. Sometimes he would take off his shirt and you could see bullet wound scars on his body. I know he was recommended for the Congressional Medal of Honor. Apparently, so the story went, the Vietcong ambushed his platoon and he was the sole survivor. When he was found, he was still alive, but had been shot several times. He was sitting with a blank stare on his face with an entrenching tool (a small shovel) in his hand. Dead Vietcong, hacked up with the entrenching tool, were found scattered all over the area. Apparently, during the firefight, Sergeant Press had run out of ammunition, so he started killing the Vietcong with the entrenching tool. When asked what happened, he looked up and said, "Hell came and Hell left." We'd heard the reason he didn't get the Congressional Medal of Honor was there were no witnesses — only his testimony. Unfortunately, it appeared that the government needed two sides to every story. It was unfortunate that he didn't receive the Congressional Medal of Honor, but the truth is, he didn't care. The only thing he cared about was the Corps and the Marines under his command. He had no other love, from what I could gather. I saw him at the Marine Corps Ball once in his Alpha uniform. He had only one ribbon, the Good Conduct Medal, on his chest. When asked where the rest of his medals were, he simply replied, "This is the only one that matters."

1st Sergeant Press was a Force Recon Marine. His sole duty was to gather intelligence. I had never seen anyone with such determination, dedication, pride, integrity, and most of all, loyalty. He was the greatest man I had ever met in my life. I am telling this story in the event any of his family is alive and perhaps reads this. It may help them understand the man and his actions. I've changed his name, but once they read the story there will be no denying his identity.

The story I am about to tell is horrendous and unthinkable, but it is also true. It gives a true meaning to Hell and the life after. I only hope the Sergeant understands that I mean no disrespect by putting his life in this book. It was included not to provide an extra chapter, but to illustrate to the American public what war actually is and what a soldier must face.

I opened up the back end of the Hummer to find 1st Sergeant Press mumbling to himself. I couldn't see well into the dark interior, so I asked, "Who's that?" Then I heard in the unmistakable voice, "Who the hell is that?" I knew right then it was 1st Sergeant Press, and he sounded drunk.

"Sergeant, it's me."

"What the hell are you doing looking in my Hum-V?"

"I'm sorry. I just heard something and was investigating. That's all. I'm leaving."

"Like hell you are, Marine! Get back here! Right now!"

I climbed in the back of the Hummer. He had a glow stick crammed in the rafters, making the lighting very poor. I could see a 9mm sitting on his right side and a Marine K-Bar knife sitting on his left, and he was, in fact, drunk. I thought this was it. He was going to kill me. I was terrified of him. He had such a mean demeanor it'd make anyone quiver. You could see the coldness and death in his eyes.

"Yes, 1st Sergeant?"

"Give me your canteen cup."

I noticed him putting something in it from a five-gallon water container. I realized that he was making his own liquor of some kind. Then he started in on me in a sarcastic tone. "So, Sergeant, you think you're a war hero over here, don't you?"

"No, 1st Sergeant."

"Yeah, you do. You all do. America has made you all heroes and you ain't seen shit."

It dawned on me that he was mad because of all the publicity we were getting, and really, we hadn't done anything to deserve it. I knew that Vietnam veterans had gotten no respect. It was shameful the way our country had treated our servicemen and women. It wasn't the fault of the men and women who participated in the war. The elected government *sent* them, and the servicemen and women got the blame. They'd done what they were told, followed their orders, and incurred the wrath from the public for their service. Of course, most of the criticism came from the cowards that wouldn't defend their own country in the first place. I suppose that's fine. Not everyone is able to serve. Those who could have participated and chose not to, well, they have to live with themselves. One thing is certain: The critics of our country and our military sure like living here.

I've never seen any of them moving out.

After getting a taste of the 1st Sergeant's wrath, I weighed my response carefully.

"1st Sergeant, I know why we are receiving all the publicity. The people in the rear now are all Vietnam vets. They're not about to let the American public criticize our troops again." For a moment, I think he actually considered my theory, but he then went back on the rampage.

"I know you hate me, and the rest of them out there do, too! You don't know shit! I wasn't always this way. I used to have fun. I had a family that loved me, but Vietnam changed all that. I am gonna tell you a story. It's about two best friends. When I'm finished, you tell me how you'd be."

I couldn't believe that this mean and intolerable old Marine was going to tell me a war story. Right from the horse's mouth! I was probably the only person he'd ever confided in. I felt honored.

"Me and my best friend decided to join the Marines together. You know, 'stead of gettin' drafted. We wanted to serve together. So off to the Marines we went. After about a year, we got sent off to Vietnam. We'd spent little over two years there when one of our missions went bad. We had about three months to go 'fore we'd be goin' home. That's when you outta be the most careful. We were Recon Marines. We received a mission to go out and gather Intel. That was the turning point of my life. We had a recon team of five personnel behind enemy lines when our cover was blown and the mission got compromised. We were bein' overrun by the Vietcong when my best friend stepped on a mine. Blew his legs off. We immediately tied tourniquets on his legs, I threw him over my shoulder, and we started runnin'. We made it 'bout two hundred yards when we realized that we weren't gonna' make it without bein' caught. We seen a culvert under a little road, so we dove down in the stream and climbed in the culvert under the road. We was lyin' there and my best friend's makin' all kinds of sounds and wouldn't keep quiet, which was understandable considerin' he just lost his legs. Well, the Vietcong was comin' and we was surly gonna get caught 'cause of my friend's noise-making, being in shock and all. We had early on made a pact: If somethin' ever happened we wouldn't let one another become prisoners of war — no matter what. My friend was almost dead from loss of blood and shock anyway, and we was about to be caught, so I decided to try to save the rest of the squad. I reached over with this K-Bar knife and cut my best friend's throat. I sat there, watchin' his blood run down the knife blade onto my hand with the blood gurgling from his throat knowin' I just killed my friend. For what? To save me and my squad. After the Vietcong left, I packed my friend over my shoulder back to camp. I went to my superiors and told them exactly what happened. Well, they weren't about to let that story out. They made up a story of how he was killed and that was that. They gave me a medal for cuttin' my best friend's throat. That's why medals don't mean shit to me."

He continued, "A few months later, they released me from the Marine Corps and sent me state-side. I went home to see my family. The first day I was back, we had a big dinner with my family and friends, and of course my best friend's family. Everyone was gathered around and wantin' me to tell stories about what had happened and I was trying' to be vague. My friend's family started talkin' about their son and wantin' to know all about him. Well, I started in with the story and one thing led to another. I couldn't take it anymore. Lyin' over my friend and all. I couldn't do it no more. I had to tell the truth. After I was done tellin' the story, everyone sat quiet. My father stood up and said he didn't know who I was, but his son died in Vietnam and that's how he was goin' to remember me. Then he turned his back to me. My mother only asked me, 'How could you have done such a thing?'

"I got up, packed my duffle bag, went to the bus stop,

went back into the Marines and requested to return to Vietnam. This time I had a new agenda. I wanted to die. I spent almost two more years over there tryin' to kill as many of the enemy as I could and die in the process. Near the end of my last hitch, I realized I wasn't gonna to die. It just wasn't in the cards, no matter what I did. So, I did my time over there until they wouldn't let me stay any longer. I came home to the states and spent the rest of my life as a Marine. I've never, ever contacted my family and they've never contacted me. I don't even know if they're alive. So, that's why I drink and that's why I've got such a pleasant personality. This here K-Bar I've been carrying around for years; I don't want to carry it no more. Sergeant, I'm givin' it to you to carry. I'll take the burden. You take the evidence."

He handed me the knife, and I took it with pride and honor. I told him if he ever wanted it back, just ask. He swore me to secrecy and I gave him my word, but his story needed to be told. The American public needs to know how ugly war is. It's not pleasant to hear, but sometimes it is necessary. They need to understand that soldiers go where our government sends them. They go nowhere of their own accord.

I sat there and listened to 1st Sergeant Press for a little while, then he went quiet and started staring off into space. I took the hint that it was time to leave. He'd said all that he had to say. It was strange. I was probably the only person that he ever told that story to. I felt privileged — and very sad — for what had happen to this brave man.

The next morning when I saw 1st Sergeant Press, it was like I'd never talked to him at all. He was as mean as ever. The only way I knew that we'd had a conversation and it wasn't just a dream was the knife that hung on my side. Later, during our deployment, I was talking to another Marine when I noticed 1st Sergeant Press staring at the knife. I wondered if he'd forgotten he gave it to me. He looked at me for a brief moment, nodded a look of approval, and moved on.

1st Sergeant Press is a man that represents what this country stands for: Pride, Integrity, Honor, Dedication, and most of all, Loyalty. His family might have turned their backs on him, but his Marine Corps family didn't. He was respected and honored. Now I understood why the mean man who stood in front of me so many times was the way he was. I was probably only one of a privileged few who had ever had conversation with him. He was a pure Marine. For him, there was no life other than the Corps.

He did talk to me one other time, just before the ground war of Desert Storm started. I was about to deploy on a mission with my squad when he came to me and said, "Sergeant, the only thing in life is your loyalty and honor. Remember that you're a Marine and only Marines can judge your actions."

I took his words of wisdom and have tried to live by them. Because of that, 1st Sergeant Press, the man that had his life taken from him, will always be a part of mine. I will always remember the time when a great warrior talked to a small pawn as an equal. I have tried to not be as quick cast judgment. I can't possibly know what another's life has endured. I hold 1st Sergeant Press in my heart with the utmost respect. I'm honored to have served with such great people. They're my family and I love and respect them all. War is hard. It changes all its participants — some for better, some for worse — and my time was coming, although I didn't know it. 1st Sergeant Press and I had one thing in common; the will to live, and at the same time, the desire to die. Death is not the mortal's choice. Only God decides.

Chapter 10
Introduction To War

After arriving in Saudi and being assigned to a battalion, the first order of business in preparing for ground war was to take a pill. We were informed this pill would help in the event we were exposed to a nerve agent. Not that I had a choice in the matter; it was either take the pill or face a court marital. The pill was called Pyriostigmine Bromide, or PB for short. The drug was given to an estimated 250,000 U.S. troops as a way to increase the effectiveness of treatment against Soman nerve agents.

PB was alleged to be FDA approved, but there were side effects. This stuff was bad. The symptoms were different for everyone, some more severe than others. I started getting severe headaches and I threw up constantly. I (and others) noticed problems with our speech and thought patterns. A classic example was trying to say a word and the spoken word would not be the word I was thinking. It was like the brain was thinking one thing and when verbalized, it out came as another. I finally realized that something was very wrong. I spoke to my Lieutenant and requested to stop taking the PB. We were forced to take a pill every morning in front of the Lieutenant. He didn't want to take it either, and decided continued medication could be voluntary. It was now totally up to each individual if we wanted to continue taking the PB.

The PB prescribed to each soldier had to be accounted for. Every morning we would pretend to take our pills, and then we'd go out and bury them. The only thing we could all agree on was that the chances for Soman gas being deployed were slim. To hell with the PB, we'd take our chances. PB is the drug that contributed to Gulf War Syndrome that you may have heard of, although the government repeatedly refused to admit any problems. You rarely hear much about Gulf War Syndrome anymore. They did their experiment, we were the guinea pigs, and hopefully that was enough.

It wasn't long until I was transferred to another battalion, and as luck would have it, my new battalion was part of a science experiment. This was one happened to be a treatment for anthrax. The treatment consisted of one shot a month for three months. Once again, it made me sick. I couldn't wait to go to transfer to another battalion and see what other experiments the military was running.

Once done with the drug testing, it was time to start the mission. I was ready. I was full of newly-minted drugs. My mind was foggy. I had headaches, diarrhea, bouts of forgetfulness, and trouble with my vision, and I couldn't think straight to save my life. I was *totally* prepared for war.

The air war started and was in full attack. We could hear the planes dropping bombs, and it was quite an eerie feeling. We would sit up all night and watch the fireworks. Then it was our turn to get bombed. We had frontline troops in foxholes about 200 yards in front of the CP (command post). The gas alarm was a hand-cranked siren, like those you have heard many times on TV — the sound of an air raid. However, this alarm wasn't used for an air raid, it was used instead for a gas attack. We had instruments to test the air for chemical agents, but the problem was that the testing equipment available didn't test for all the different types of chemical weapons we might encounter.

There are four basic types of chemical weapons:

1.) Nerve Agents — These are deployed as gas or liquid. If deployed as a gas, the amount of time it will stay in the area is dependent upon temperature and sunlight. Liquid form will stay a lot longer. Nerve agents can be deployed by artillery or plane. Take one breath and you start to die. It basically turns your insides out. Your body bends in a fashion it's not meant to. There is a cure, it's called 2 Pan Chloride and Atropine. Each Marine is giving three injection needles of each. If you are exposed, you inject the antidote into your thigh, but first you must remember to get your gas mask on. You could possibly live if you move fast enough. Last but not least, the gas is colorless and odorless, making it impossible to recognize except by seeing one of your fellow Marines stricken with the symptoms.

2.) Blister Agents — A blister agent (aka: a vesicant) is a chemical compound that causes severe skin, eye, and mucosal pain and irritation. Sulfur Mustard is a family of sulfur-based agents, including the so-called "mustard gas" you may have heard of. These chemicals are named for their ability to cause large, painful water blisters on the bodies of affected individuals. Although these compounds have been employed for medical purposes, their most common use is chemical warfare. This agent is not designed to kill, but rather to remove large numbers of soldiers from the battle for a while. One drop of this will cause about a half-dollar size blister and pain to go along with it. It has the smell of almonds.

3.) Blood Agents — A blood agent (aka: cyanogen agent) is a chemical compound carried by the blood for distribution through the body. They may contain the cyanide group, which can deactivate the energy-producing enzymes of cells in the body. They are misnamed because these agents don't typically affect the blood, though they may interrupt the production of blood components. They exert toxic effects at the cellular level. Blood agents can all act upon tissues in the body once distributed by the blood. There is no cure. Once exposed, you die. These agents are deployed by artillery or plane, and always as a gas, so they tend to not stay in an area too long.

4.) Choking Agents — Phosgene kills any breathing thing by attacking the lung capillaries and then the membranes of the lung sacs. It causes the lungs to flood with fluids. If exposed, death can follow in mere hours, or can take up to a day. Phosgene is particularly dangerous because it doesn't detoxify naturally. It has a cumulative effect on its victims and can linger in sheltered areas and buildings. It has the smell of freshly-cut grass. There is no cure. You die a horrible death, puking your guts up.

During the first Gulf War, we knew Saddam had nerve agents and mustard gas. Once the alarm went off, we all suit up in chemical protective gear, including gas masks. The gear is called MOPP (Mission Oriented Protective Posture). There is only a small amount of time a person can stay suited up. The reasons are, 1.) it is extremely hot and you will dehydrate fast if you don't drink lots of fluids (the gas mask is equipped with a drinking tube so you can drink out of your canteen without exposing yourself to the gas); and 2.) you have to evacuate the area because the suits are only good for approximately 12 hours of exposure.

Once the testing equipment indicates that the gas has cleared the area, you go to step two of detection. The lowest ranking man is disarmed and told they are going to test for gas in the area. He is instructed to remove his gas mask, open his eyes, then put the mask back on and clear it. At this time he is observed for any symptoms of exposure. If no symptoms are present, remove the mask, take one breath, put the mask back on and clear it. Again observe for symptoms of exposure. Last, remove the mask and breath normally until given the sign for all clear. While the mask is off, observe for symptoms for 20 minutes. This might sound cruel, but one person dying can save many more lives. That's one of the chances you take being a low rank.

The first night we received artillery attack, someone

gave the signal for gas. The alarm went off and we suited up. We immediately tried to confirm what type of gas was deployed, who sounded the alarm, and why. Our detectors showed nothing, but, like I said, the detectors didn't recognize all types of gas and we couldn't find who sounded the alarm. It was chaos. It was dark, hot, and we were burning up. I would say we had been in the suits for about four hours, and it was starting to take a toll on everyone. The Colonel told the 1st Sgt. go get a Private. I knew what that meant. Someone was about to take off their gas mask.

They brought in a Private, took his weapon, sat him down, and explained what was about to take place. Needless to say, the Private started crying and pleading with the group of men around him. He was scared, and rightfully so. I couldn't stand it. If someone was going to be the first chemical agent casualty, it was me. I felt I had earned it, he hadn't. It was my time to shine, I wanted the recognition for being a hero. So I did what I had to. While everyone focused on talking to the Private, I took off my mask and stood in the background. I walked up to the 1st Sergeant and asked if I could get a MRE (Meals Ready to Eat). I was hungry. Everyone else was in shock, watching me stand there asking for food with no gas mask. At first, everyone just looked confused. I repeated the question. I was hungry, going to go get an MRE, and wondered if anyone else wanted one. Most people knew my sense of humor, but some didn't, and they were trying to tell me to get my mask on. I told them I had already had it off for five minutes, and I thought it was safe. For the next few months the alarm would go off periodically. Everyone would go nuts and I would walk around without my gear. I did get into trouble for not taking it seriously, but who cares? I remember walking into the CP one time, when everyone was fully suited up. I ate crackers and asked when we had changed our uniforms to these ugly ones. Call it dumb. Call it crazy. I call it leading by example. Besides, they recommended me for a nice big medal.

We received our orders to jump 20 miles south of Kuwait. We were to do a land area reconnaissance, gathering Intel for Task Force Ripper. Our main objective was to find a nice passage into the outskirts of Kuwait. Once our journey was completed, the task force would then proceed up to our objective. If something went wrong, we could immediately request a chopper for evacuation. Overall, the mission should have been a nice, easy, two-day affair...but nothing ever goes as planned.

At 0000 hours we were packed and ready to climb into a CH-46 helicopter for our morning jump. As we climbed in, Hodge look at me and said, "Finger, I feel like I'm not comin' back. I'm gonna die in this godforsaken place."

I reassured him that the area had already been cleared by helicopters and aerial surveillance. Everything was routine. He looked at me with some sign of relief and followed me into the chopper. I looked at the other members of my squad — Hodge, Moon-pie and Somali. We were snipers and the best squad in the unit. I think the reason we all got along was that we left each other alone to make our own judgments on things, unless someone specifically asked. We were all-stubborn, and no one else wanted us in their squad. We were unique.

We were all Marines through and through. We sat in the chopper as it started to take off. I looked at the ground as it started to get smaller, wondering what we were getting ourselves into. After reaching 12,000 feet the chopper pilot told us to put on our oxygen masks and prepare for the jump. The crew chief came, tied himself in, and opened the back door to the chopper. As it lowered I could see only the black of night. The green light to go lit. I stepped off first and fell through the sky like a rock. I rolled to look for my partners but couldn't see anything. I looked at my altimeter gauge. At 1,000 feet, I pulled my main chute. As I waited for the canopy to open I thought, *This is it. I hope Hodge's instinct isn't correct.*

As I fell I heard a "woof" sound, indicating my canopy was all the way open. Soon I would be slowing to a falling speed that could be maintained. I heard my friend's chutes — pop, pop and pop — and I knew we had all made successful jumps and we would all soon be on the ground. I watched as the earth came closer and closer. I would soon be stepping onto what I thought was secure ground. Little did I know...

I landed on the ground safely and turned see my three compadres landing within 100 feet of me. I took off my chute and held my M-4 at the ready, waiting for anything to make a move. Unfortunately, we were in the wide open. We were sitting ducks if someone was dug in, even in the dark.

After we were all secure, we packed up our chutes and buried them (so no one would discover our presence), taking a bearing from the GPS so we could return to the spot and retrieve them later. We gathered up and talked about the path we were going to follow, and got our heading. Everyone agreed and off we went.

After about one hour of walking with our NVGs (night vision goggles) on, I stepped on what sounded like wood. I raised my fist to stop everyone and we stood there for a minute to look around. I heard the sound of snoring. We stood there in awe wondering, *What the hell is this*? This place was supposed to be clear of Iraqis, and we were walking on one of their bunkers! The wood that I stepped on must have been there to cover a foxhole.

I made the signal to slowly back up and move to the side. As I was backing up I could hear movement, but there was no one in sight. After moving back about 30 yards, we made a circle around the camp to get an idea of how many could possibly be at this checkpoint. There were no vehicles of any kind, and this spot couldn't be seen from the air. It was well concealed. This led me to believe that our intelligence was either not doing their job, or was just leading us into this pit. I thought it funny that we were dropped off at that given point, told to go in a specific direction, and just happened to find an Iraqi bunker. It might have been just a coincidence, but I'll never know.

Moon-pie tapped me on the shoulder, giving me the signal to get down. I slowly moved to the ground, watching what seemed to be an Iraqi coming out of the bunker. I brought my gun to the ready as I lay in the sand waiting for hell to break out. Our plan, if something like this happened, was to overrun their entrances, toss grenades in the holes, and take them out as they came out into the open. We lay in the sand with our NVGs glued to this guy taking a whiz in the sand. I thought it strange that there was no sentry. *Why are these guys here? Why aren't they concerned about us?* If they were, they didn't act like it. The Iraqi finished his piss and went back into his foxhole. Using the GPS, I recorded the exact, pinpoint location of the position. By the size of the trenches and foxhole covers, we estimated there were no more than 10-20 Iraqis.

We started back in our direction of pursuit again, wondering what we would uncover next. It was getting to be about 0230, when we noticed a large object in the distance about one mile from the bunker. It appeared to be some kind of vehicle. The closer we got, the bigger it got. I told the squad we should not in engage in any type of activity unless we had no choice. They agreed. We fell into single-file to make our size look smaller, and made our way to the vehicle.

At about 100 yards out, we could clearly see the vehicle was an Iraqi T-62 tank. Not a good sight for four guys on the ground with only small arms. For some strange reason we kept going, but we all agreed something didn't look right. As we got closer, we could see the tank had been blown up. Collectively, our breathing became more settled. I stepped forward and heard a cracking sound as my foot landed. Looking down, I could see my foot had gone clean

134

through a burned Iraqi man's chest. He must have been pretty burned, had been there for a while, or both.

We continued on, recording all that we found; two more bodies inside the tank, some papers that looked like some kind of mapping, possibly mapped bunkers. We took GPS readings and started on our way again.

We kept moving until about 0430. In the distance, we again noticed something strange. There appeared to be road signs of some sort, but we weren't aware of any roads near our current location. As we proceeded, we noticed three individuals standing out in the open. We dropped to the ground and watched from about 200 yards out. With the moonlit background, we could clearly see them, but something was very strange about these personnel. They weren't moving in any particular direction, and had been standing in the exact same spot for at least 30 minutes.

"Hodge, something ain't right. Moon-pie, you and Somali circle 'round. Hodge and I will move up and see what is goin' on up there," I whispered.

As the other two circled, Hodge and I made our way slowly forward, and the closer we got, I began to identify the most gruesome sight I'd ever seen to this point in my life. I stood, mouth agape, looking at three men impaled with re-bar; the thick metal rods had been rammed through their asses and exited through their mouths. They had been impaled and stuck in the sand like road signs. I was in awe. My partners talked softly about the kind of animals were we dealing with as the bodies of the three men stared back at us like macabre scarecrows.

I voiced a quick decision. "Don't let 'em take me prisoner! It's all or nothin'. No POW shit for me."

We all agreed and the pact was struck.

After what seemed an eternity, we started moving. The sun was about to be up. We needed to make cover for a little while, organize our observations, and call in a report of our findings and coordinates. We walked about two miles until we could see the sun starting to rise. Moon-pie suggested we dig in and call it a night. I agreed. We had just started digging our holes when we heard choppers coming. We knew one thing — they had to be ours. We continued to dig as the sound of the rotors came closer and closer. I told my companions to keep digging and I'd call in our position, just in case. I didn't want to become a casualty of friendly fire.

I called in our position, told them that choppers were in our immediate area, and requested the aircraft move out in order not to compromise our position. The radio operator told me to hold and they'd get back to me in a few minutes. I went back to my digging and soon the radio started talking again, requesting a report of anything seen. I reminded the radio control operator, "That information is for Colonel Coe only. Recon 1 out."

1st Sergeant Press came over the radio, "Recon 1— report!"

I reported our findings and all the coordinates. There was a pause on the other end. I assumed he was taking notes or thinking about what we had encountered. The 1st Sergeant came back on the radio, "Recon 1, dig in at your present location, observe for the day, report any movement throughout the day and move out at dusk."

We finished the foxholes, each about four feet deep. We covered each hole with a poncho to conceal it and provide shade. The ponchos were the color of sand, so seeing one from the air would be difficult. We sat in the two foxholes yakking to each other. After a while, Hodge, my foxhole buddy, decided it was necessary for him to take a dump. Anyone who has read this far is aware of the bathroom procedure for foxhole living. Moon-pie and Somali started laughing. They knew I had to sit there, watch and smell. So I sat, watching my friend use the bathroom, and thought this job just wasn't worth it sometimes. But I knew it wouldn't be long before I had to do the same. What comes around goes around. The humor my two currently unaffected companions got out of this situation, and their ensuing comments, only made it worse. When their time came, I hoped I was awake, because they were getting it back in spades.

We sat around telling stories of our lives, things we'd done and things we'd gone through. Hodge told a story of he and I stealing all the M&Ms from the officers MRE stash when we were on radio comms for the unit. Since only one in 10 MREs had M&Ms in them, we had to go through about 150 MREs to get 15 bags of M&Ms. The next morning some Lieutenant came in complaining that someone had broken into all the MREs and stolen all the M&Ms. We denied it, but almost got ourselves into a lot of trouble.

I told the story of my first encounter with a camel. We had been in the Brakon oil fields. Because all the black smoke from the burning oil, night vision was impossible. I'd been up for two days without sleep. Finally, it was my turn for a little nap. It was about midnight and there was a high wind that night. At that time, I didn't have a foxhole, so I decided I'd sleep next to a Hummer in order to get out of the wind. I put my sleeping bag next to the tire and lay down with my weapon on my chest. After about 10 minutes, something hit me in the head. I thought it was one of the guys using the butt of his rifle to wake me up. I'd just gotten comfortable and didn't want to get up, so I acted like I hadn't woken up. WHAM! Another smack to the head again. I threw my sleeping bag open, looked up to start bitching, and I saw a camel straddling me. Apparently the Hummer made a good windbreak for the camel, too. I took my M-4 and hit him in the stomach. The camel took off, hitting me on the head with his knee. I tried to get a bead on him to kill him, but couldn't see anything but stars. That camel kicked me so hard in the head I almost passed out. For a while in the unit, it was "Bob the camel jockey," "Bob the camel-lover," or "Bob and the camel" this or that. It took a while for the hazing to subside.

We sat around, slept, and told stories, waiting for nightfall so we could finish our ground survey of the area. As the day went on, the stories got funnier. The four of us were actually having a good time laughing and recalling all the things that had happened in our lives, just like four old friends who hadn't seen each other in years. At about 1700 hours, we heard the sounds of choppers — choppers and their Gatling guns — in the direction of the Iraqi bunker that we discovered. I immediately called in. The radio operator told us to stand by.

Within an hour, Colonel Coe came on the radio and gave us our new orders. I should have known what they were going to be. "Go clear the bunker, and I mean clear it!"

We took that to mean kill anyone left and gather anything that could be pertinent to our operations. That meant checking for maps, paperwork, or anything that looked important — like we could tell. None of us could read Arabic. We sat there and thought about what the Colonel had said. I was excited.

Hodge piped up, "Well, Bob, now's time for the psycho to come front and center."

"This is different, Hodge! Look what they did to their own! If anyone deserves to die, it's them!"

Hodge gave it a rest and we made our plan of attack.

The plan was for us to go in 30 to 40 yards apart, try to circle the camp, and kill whatever moved. We could see at night — we prayed they couldn't. We'd start by throwing grenades into the holes, if there were any left from the choppers, sit and wait for movement, and take them out. First we'd make sure to and do a recon of the site from a distance. We didn't want to walk into a trap with only a four-man squad.

I keyed in the coordinates and pinpointed our location five miles from the site. We decide to take off at about 1900 hours. We had one hour to make preparations and clean up our site, so as to leave no trace of our presence.

We started off heading in the direction of the camp. We were all thinking about what was about to happen. I don't believe any of us were really ready for what might be in store. We made our way within 200-300 yards of the site and lay down to make observations. We expected to see vehicles coming with reinforcements, but there was nothing. This meant either they had no radio comms to let anyone know they were hit, or they were all dead. Regardless, we decided to wait and watch for movement.

We waited about 30 minutes and there wasn't any kind of movement. We decided to move in closer for a better vantage point. About 50 yards out, we crouched down to make our final spot check. We were just about to get up when Hodge gave me the signal that he had spotted something. I looked, but couldn't make anything out. Then Somali made the acknowledge signal, indicating that he saw it, too.

I whispered, "Hodge, what is it?"

"Looks like someone's moving, lying on the ground."

"Let's watch for a moment, then get this over with."

Hodge passed the info down the line.

I continued to watch the area where Hodge and Somali had indicated movement. It wasn't long until I noticed an arm reach up and make a slight move for a moment.

I passed the word to the squad, "Let's do it. Assume all have weapons and kill anything that moves."

We advanced slowly toward the bunkers. We each took a side as we approached, then moved in fast. Gunfire broke out and I heard the sound of grenades going off. Moon-pie killed the Iraqi that we'd seen moving. I started in on the far bunker, throwing grenades into the caved-in roof. As quickly as it started, it was over. In fact, there wasn't even a fight. The only person that seemed to be alive was the one Iraqi we'd seen prior to moving in. We started setting up stations, looking and trying to hear any movement. There was none. It appeared the choppers had finished the job they started.

Next, we cleared all bunkers as best as we could in the dark. There were three. We took turns, two standing guard while the other two of us cleared the bunker.

The first bunker, where the one Iraqi had been alive, was partially caved in. Moon-pie and Somali cleared the bunker while Hodge and I kept guard on the other two. Somali went in, followed by Moon-pie. After about five minutes, Somali came out.

"Nothin' but pieces, Finger. Best I can tell, maybe three people, but nothing alive."

Hodge and I went in to clear the second bunker. Most of it was caved in, so we started to shovel our way in while the others stood watch. After about an hour, we could make out the entrance. We looked in — nothing. It appeared to be an ammo bunker.

Somali and I decide to clear the last bunker. We had to squeeze through the entrance, but we got in. We found some small mortars and what seemed to be large range artillery pieces. What we initially thought to be 10-20 personnel turned out to be, maybe, a four-man outpost.

Once we'd seen and cleared the area it was time to call in and report the findings. We made our way to bunker #1 and set up. I picked up the radio and called the dispatcher.

"Task Force Ripper, come in. This is Recon 1, over."

"Recon 1, stand by for Recon Bravo."

Recon Bravo meant 1st Sergeant Press.

"Recon 1, this is Recon Bravo and Alfa. Report!"

I gave the report and waited for instructions.

"Recon 1, you are to remain there until morning. Get an accurate count of all inventory, ammo, and body counts. Once everything is accounted for, we will make our decision about destroying it or leaving for the si-ops (Scientific Investigative Operations) to come and investigate."

"Roger, Recon 1 out."

Now we had to stay and set up camp among the dead. We quickly made a sweep of the area in order to place ourselves in the most strategic position. If more personnel came out of hiding, or if a rescue unit showed up, we were stuck. We had to be prepared to defend our position against who knew what. We got together and made a group call. We decided to use the #2 bunker as our main post. If someone did come, there was extra ammo, grenades, and who knew what else in there. As an added benefit, there were no dead bodies in #2. We also decided no one would sleep that night. We did what we could to make our little hole less vulnerable for a possible attack. Hodge and I started making improvements while Somali and Moon-pie went over to bunker #1 to collect the extra weapons they had seen. They returned with three AK-47s, a pistol, and lots of ammo.

Moon-pie smiled and added, "We found some food and water, if you want it."

I said definitely not. He was kidding, anyway. While Hodge and I continued reinforcing our bunker, Moon-pie and Somali went back to bunker #1 to see what else they could dig up. Their second trip produced a cornucopia of goodies, in case we needed them — land mines, grenades, mortar rounds and some type of long range artillery rounds. All that was left to do was hold down the fort for several hours, wait for daylight, and make an accurate assessment of the area.

I don't know what came over us that night but we joked and laughed just as loud as we wanted. There could have been enemy right on top of us, but we acted like we didn't care. We stayed up talking about everything, even the dead Iraqis 20 feet away. One of our main topics was food. We all wanted a pizza or Taco Bell or McDonald's. It's funny how the things you take for granted turn out to be the foremost thoughts of happier times. As the night rolled on, we sat around and told stories again, while each of us dozed off now and then. We all seemed quite content with napping in the graveyard. It's odd how you can grow accustomed to such things. For a while, we joked the dead Iraqis were coming back, but that's as far as it went.

Morning came and we started moving around, anxiously waiting for dawn so we could scout out the area. Our first thought was to go in, take cover, and keep our eyes open in case of surprises. That's what we did. I called in to camp, let them know we were still alive and well, and we were about to commence scouting. I also made a point to make sure to let all choppers know we were in the area.

Upon our final surveillance, we found that bunkers # 2 and 3 were empty. The dead in bunker #1 were more apparent in the daylight. The first dead Iraqi, the one Moonpie had shot, was blown almost in half. How he managed to stay alive so long was mystery. He was dead now and I am sure he had welcomed it. There were more bodies than we'd previously thought. Four bodies were inside. Human remains lay all over, scattered from one end to the other. The chopper's Gatling guns had blown through the wooden top of the bunker and killed everyone inside — more than once.

It was a mission — one of many — I wouldn't easily forget.

Chapter 11

Combat

The day finally came for us to earn our pay. I can remember looking at my three friends as we started for the C-130. Hodge was in his finest hour — a man on a mission. Moon-pie was a mean Marine with a look of determination to protect life and country. Who could forget Somali's face? A look would make even the Devil shiver. And then there was me. I couldn't see my face, but I am sure there was no expression. I was only determined to get my death count higher.

We loaded up on the plane. Our destination was Kuwait City. We were to do a recon, radio back to the task force, and wait for instruction. I didn't know that it was a one-way ticket to Hell, and in some respects, there was no coming back. At the time, I looked at it another way. I believe Revelations 6:8 said it best: *And I looked, and behold a pale horse: and his name that sat on him was Death...* Unfortunately it was Saddam who was on the horse, not me.

At 0200, we boarded the C-130 plane.

"Hodge, you ready?"

"Yeah, more than ever. It's finally time to get my name in this history book."

I looked at him. All I saw was determination. He didn't even look nervous.

"Hodge, you think we'll make it?"

"Does it matter?"

"Guess not. I was just wonderin' what you're feeling."

"Put it like this; if my chute doesn't open, it was meant to be; if it does, then that was meant to be."

"Talk about living for the moment."

We both laughed.

I leaned by his ear, touched him on the shoulder, and said, "Your family would be very proud of you."

He looked at me and said the same.

I pulled the squad together and talked through the plans one more time.

"All right, once we land on the outskirts of Kuwait, we will bury our chutes and mark the site with our GPS. Then we'll do a radio check to Bald Eagle 1 — Colonel Coe. After that, we make sure nothing fell off on the jump. Each one of us does a personnel check and buddy check."

A buddy check is something done in the military to double-check each other. In time of confusion and stress, it is easy to overlook something trivial or important. We had already double-checked each other, but during a parachute jump, it's easy to lose something in the fall.

"Once we do our checks and radio check, we will proceed to Destination One."

Destination One was just outside the south side of Kuwait City.

Our items of a carry were:

- M40 Sniper rifle — 7.62, maximum effective range 800 meters; if you're good, 1000 meters. Ammo — as much as you can carry, typically, 50-100 rounds.
- M9 Pistol — 9mm, 4 mags and 50 extra rounds. Used only as a back-up to your main weapon, not a self-defense weapon.
- Assault weapon — primary weapon of movement. Can be MP-5, M-4, M-16 or, possibly, AK-47. Spec Ops allows individual choice. Ammo — as much as possible, 200-400 rounds.
- M-97 fragmentation grenades — to get you out of the area.
- Incendiary grenade — gives off several thousand degrees of heat. Used to melt the sniper rifle in the event you are overrun. Renders the weapon inoperable.

144

- Color smoke grenade — lets the friendlies know where you or the enemy is.
- Range finder
- NVGs (Night Vision Goggles)
- Medical bag
- Radio
- Knife, Leatherman multi-tool, food, water, gas mask
- One hollow tip 9mm bullet — for yourself.

All of this stuff is heavy, but it makes for a good hunting trip. After much deliberation, we were about to jump into the black abyss and make our way to the south side of Kuwait City near the airport. The light turned red, telling us that we were getting ready to jump. We were making a HALO (High Altitude Low Opening) jump. When you jump, you don't want to hang in the air and be a target. Your chute is pulled at low altitude, 800 feet or so. If you pull too late, the canopy won't have time to open and slow you down, so of course, you'll hit hard.

Somali went first. The light turned green and I patted him on the butt. Then Moon-pie and Hodge, each receiving a tap on the behind from me when cleared to jump. I was last. The crew chief tapped my behind and out the door I went. The night was made even blacker with smoke from the Al Burgan oil fields. Very little light could be seen from Kuwait City. As I dropped through the darkness, thoughts flew through my head. *Is this death? Are we coming back?* And most of all, *I hope I don't become a POW.*

The ground came up all too soon. Poof! My chute deployed. I couldn't see the others, but heard each one check in. I hugged my assault rifle at my side, ready for whatever happened. I landed softly in the dry sand and quickly started wrapping up my chute for storage. We all met up and dug a shallow grave for the chutes. After marking the area with our GPS, we headed off toward the few dim lights we could see in the distance.

We made good time. About 300 yards from town, we came to our first empty enemy bunker. I motioned for Hodge and Moon-pie to check the bunker while Somali and I stayed up to provide cover. Hodge came back first.

"Finger, I think you otta see this."

That wasn't a good sign. As I approached, a disgusting smell caught my attention. Hodge shined his light into the bunker and my eyes caught sight of the rotting corpse of a woman that had been tacked against the wall. The body was cut innumerable times from head to toe. It appeared that she had been used as a target in some sinister, repulsive game of darts.

"What kind of people are these?" I muttered.

Somali smiled and said, "Dead."

We made our way out of the bunker, trying not to puke from the smell and what we had just seen. Once out, we started for town. We made it to the edge of the city before we noticed any people. Not Iraqis, but Kuwaitis — at least I thought. I told the squad that we needed to get to high cover and start our reconnaissance of the area before daylight came. There was a building that Intel had told us was deserted, and we were supposed to get to it. We had maps, but from the look of things, a change in plans came to my mind.

It was worst mistake of my life.

Light was coming and the building seemed miles away — but in actuality, it was only maybe 700 yards. We came around a corner, trying to stay off the walls as much as possible to avoid bullet ricochet. As we made our way along, a woman looked out her door, saw us, and went back inside. My heart was pumping so fast that I could hear my own pulse. We came upon a narrow road that had two sets of stairs on each side of the street. The stairs went up the sides of each of the buildings. For some reason, there were two concrete walls on either side of the street, each about three feet wide. Looking down the street, you could see on one side a three-foot wall going to the top of the building, and on the other side you would see the same thing.

About 100 yards out, all hell broke out. Someone took a shot at us. Hodge and I went to the one side of the building and climbed the stairs while Moon-pie and Somali went up the other building's stairs. The war was on. Fire was coming from down range at us as we hurried to the top. It looked like 30-40 personnel were hiding behind the two walls, shooting at us.

I made it to the top and started returning fire, giving my buddies cover to safe passage. Once we all safely reached the top, we were in position to fight back. We were out-manned, and in short order, surrounded. Our positions had the enemy in a crossfire and death was coming. I could see them across the road. Somali could surely see them across the other way. I started shooting. It was like shooting sitting ducks. They kept shooting at us as we sat there picking them off. The body count was going up. It was as easy as hitting a barn door with a shotgun. The fury and adrenalin was pumping. I was killing with Hodge. I couldn't see what Somali & Moon-pie were doing, but our side was catchin' hell. The fire just kept coming. It seemed like an eternity, but actually it was maybe only a few minutes. I knew it wouldn't be long before they came after us from the backside. I couldn't believe these Iraqis were so stupid as to try to hide behind the three-foot wall and shoot at us! I sat there with Hodge and laughed at their ignorance. It was a feeding frenzy for us. I couldn't believe how they let us shoot them down.

One Iraqi made the grave mistake of attempting to get to the other side of the wall. I shot him in the waist. Maybe it was to torture him for the woman in the bunker, or maybe I thought I could bait the others out. He dropped and was trying to crawl to the other side when I let another go. The round caught him in the shoulder. He lay and screamed. I needed him immobilized. As he lay screaming, my plan

147

began to work. One of the others tried to stretch out to help. Hodge shot that guy in the chest. He fell dead.

"Nice shot, Hodge!"

I could see a man's shoulder sticking out as he tried to stay covered. I shot him in the shoulder. He fell and tried to cover himself, but it was too late. Hodge finished him off. One brought them out, the other finished them off. This strategy was working well. It was too easy.

Moon-pie and Somali were taking turns on the others. They probably had just as many down as we did. I brought my focus back to the fight. I noticed the guy on the ground wasn't getting enough attention, so I shot him again. This time I took out his knee. Damn, that must have hurt! It worked, because someone came running across from the other side to drag him to the wall. That didn't last. The other sniper team took him out. He dropped on top his injured partner. The bodies started piling up.

We had the Iraqis pinned down behind the walls. They could have run backwards and tried their luck in getting back to the street, but it appeared none of them wanted to take that chance. Time had slowed down. Periodically, they would stick their weapons around the wall and fire them sporadically. What a joke!

"Hodge, we need to get around behind and finish them off!"

"The only way to get 'em all is to get them out in the open, Finger!"

"I will keep 'em covered; you go 'round and take a peek!"

After his quick recon, Hodge reported back.

"The only way is to jump to the other building. It's too far! If we were gonna do it, we would have to climb down the stairs and make our way 'round. Not a good idea to leave our post just yet," he reported.

"We need some way to draw them out in the open, and one of us needs to keep an eye on our backs. I'll keep these guys pinned down; you make sure that our rear ain't bein' compromised!" I said.

Hodge turned to face our backs and kept a close eye out. I kept on firing as the opportunity arose.

As the firefight died down, I saw a handheld rocket come whistling by. *What the hell was that?* I heard a loud explosion that rocked the earth, and pieces of stone were flying through the air. I squatted down and looked back at Hodge, who was lying flat on the roof. I sat for a minute so my mind could settle in. Then I thought, *Holy shit!* I looked up and over to see Moon-pie and Somali... gone! I couldn't believe my eyes!

"Hodge, they're gone! They're gone!"

"Who's gone?"

They're gone! Moon-pie and Somali! They're blown to pieces!"

Hodge and I started to lay down fire. I was shooting the wall and everything else in sight. They were firing all around us now. The ones behind the other wall were spraying us with bullets. This whole damn thing was getting out of control.

"Hodge, they're now on their way around the building to get us from the back! We need to do something now! Call in the helos! We need a way to get out of this shit! Get on the radio and call for backup! Let 'em know we're in deep!"

I continued firing at will. At the rate I was going, I'd be out of ammo soon. I could hear Hodge in the background calling in, but with all the commotion I couldn't hear everything. I finally had enough. We needed to get the hell out.

"Hodge, we got to go!"

There was no reply. I glanced back to see my friend lying lifeless. Life was suddenly moving in slow motion. I looked over at him and saw all the blood. Hodge had been shot through the neck. I grabbed Hodge and tried to administer aid, but it was too late. He was dead. I sat down and hugged my friend.

"Hodge, you need to wake up! I need your help to get out of here! Hodge, please!"

Hodge was dead.

I was alone and surrounded by these animals. They had taken out my friends and now they were after me. I looked down just in time to see a rope being thrown across the road. *What the hell are they doing now?* A rocket launcher was tied to the rope and being dragged back across. They needed it on the other side to shoot at me. I took my rifle and shot the trigger-housing unit, demobilizing the launcher.

Time was getting short. I either had to make a stand, or run for it. I knew if I stayed it would only be a matter of time before I was surrounded and they'd finish me off. The only reasonable choice was to run. I took out an incendiary grenade and placed it on the receiver section of my sniper rifle. An incendiary grenade burns at 1000° F, melting the weapon, so no one can ever use it again. I only had a few shells left and everything from here on out was going to be close order anyway. I melted my weapon, and gathered ammo and water from Hodge's body. I took one last look at my buddy and at the blood. The last reminder of Hodge's life was stained on my shirt. He'd given his life — and now his remaining supplies — for me. All I had left of my friend were the blotches of crimson on my uniform.

I took off. I ran as fast as I could to the other side of the building and peeked over the side. Nothing. A pole ran up the side of the building. I started down the pole as fast as I could, attempting to make as little noise as possible. As I was going down, I could hear the Iraqis screaming at the top. They must have found Hodge's body.

I made it down to the street and was off. I ran until I came upon a trashed plane. It must have been a 747 or something similar. It was blown apart in the middle and looked like a good place to sit and think for a minute. I ran into the plane to catch my breath and take a look. Surprisingly, there was no one on board, dead or alive. I sat there for just a few minutes. I could hear a lot of commotion coming my way, and I knew that sitting inside this plane was not the ideal situation for combat. I needed an edge, and this wasn't it. A quick look around revealed what I thought to be the airport terminal. The building was blown apart, and part of the side had been destroyed, but it could give me some concealment and cover. I made my way to the building and slowly pushed the door open, not knowing whether this would be my tomb or my salvation. It would take me three days to find out.

Chapter 12

Hell on Earth – Kuwait City Airport, Day 1

I slowly moved around the corner and considered my current status. I was alone in the middle of the Kuwaiti airport. All of my friends were dead and now the Iraqis were looking for me. Working my way through the airport, I approached the Kuwait International Hotel. It didn't take a discerning eye to realize that it had seen better days. Half of the building had been blown to pieces, but the other half still looked intact. I grabbed my MP-5 and made my way to the building. As I made my way inside, I saw a large wooden ship sitting inside a glass enclosure. It was a strange, beautiful sight in the midst of all the destruction. But what I came across next, I'd just as soon forget.

In the lobby area, a very pretty little girl, I guessed about 10 years old, wearing a blue dress, lay on her back with her small little legs spread open. One of her legs was tied to the stairway handrail, the other had been tied with a rope to something that must have been parked outside. This child had likely been raped, probably an ungodly amount of times, then tied to the staircase and pulled apart like a Sunday dinner wishbone. Her body was almost in half. Her face was what really got me. Her eyes were staring into some far-off place, expressionless. Her mouth told the rest of the story. It was open, as if frozen in a scream — a scream for her young life which no one heard. As I looked down I could see that she had dug her fingernails so far into her own hand that she caused blood to start pouring from her palms. It's the expression on that angelic face that will never leave my mind. Humans were not meant to witness such atrocities. These were the animals I faced. The pain this child must have felt! What god would have permitted it? Why? If this had been a military combatant, I could have understood, but why put such a small, innocent child through such horrors? My blood started to boil.

I made my way up the staircase, looking for some kind of refuge until the Marines got there. I had three days to wait. Making my way to the third floor, I came upon an Iraqi sitting and looking out a window. He had a knife, but no gun. I didn't want to shoot and risk making a noise that might alert any others. I made a slight sound and he turned. It wasn't much of a fight. Gripping my rifle, I struck him in the head. I felt his skull give way under the blow of the rifle butt, but I continued hitting him with the butt of my rifle until his crushed scull was showing its contents. The extra blows had been unnecessary, but the only thing going through my mind was the little girl. I kept striking the man with everything I had, even though I knew he was dead. As aggressively as I started, I stopped. A thought came to my mind changed my life. *The inhumanity of man really brings out the godliness in others*. I didn't want to be like the people that had killed the little girl downstairs, and yet that's what I had become. I leaned over the body of the dead man and whispered, "I'm sorry." Had he not wanted to fight for some reason? He seemed to let me kill him with no resistance. Why? That was a question that would haunt me for the rest of my life.

I made my way over to the elevator. It was obviously out of commission, but I thought it would give me a good place to hide and think. Taking my K-bar, I wedged it in the doors and pried them open. There was no elevator, only cables. I looked down to see the elevator sitting about 10 feet below me. I positioned myself inside. Holding onto the cables, I finally got the doors shut and slid down to the top of the elevator. Maybe not the best place to be, but it was a suitable hideout for a while. I checked my supplies. I had one and a half canteens of water and part of a MRE.

What to do now? I had three days to sit, not make a sound, and survive in 100° heat with only a small portion of water. I was scared, and I wasn't accustomed to it. I didn't want to end up a POW of these people! They hadn't any ethical code of conduct. They didn't obey the rules. We treated enemy prisoners with a measure of respect, fed them, gave medical aid, and such. A U.S. soldier gets caught, and off goes our head! And the beatings — I didn't want to go there. I had my plan. If they found me, I wouldn't become a POW. My last act in the fight would be to take my own life. That was that.

I felt very alone. No other feeling ever came. I felt alone, lost, and forgotten. I had some sense of what the Vietnam vets felt, though I didn't compare my current little misery to what they went through. But I had a taste of it. I felt sick inside. ***The pain and suffering that war brings out. Why can't we have peace? With humans, it's not possible. We're always at war with someone. Peace is only a word invented to cover up the lies for what is really behind each war.*** The feeling of being left behind is inexplicable. I could write volumes attempting to convey it and still not come close. The only way to know is to be there, and actually wonder if your life is about over. I sat on top of an inoperable elevator, listening to people speaking Arabic right outside the doors. Feeling that life is near its end is detrimental to your health. I had never been afraid of anything, much less dying, but now, when it was so close and death was facing me, I was scared. ***Why?*** I had come to realize I had not been a paladin, but a blinded, psychotic killer. I had been given permission for my actions under rules of law — but who in a government were they to hand down judgments of life and death? There was only one who had that power, and I didn't even know Him. A chaplain once told me there were no atheists in foxholes. Now I knew it wasn't an old cliché. Oh, how I believed him now! ***Is it too late for me***? That was the question that went through my

mind over and over. *__Will God forgive my actions — my__*
__blind, misguided, actions?__

I don't believe I ever would have had those thoughts
if it weren't for the little girl and the man I'd beaten so
unmercifully. *__Did God put me in this situation in order to__*
__teach me a lesson in humanity? Was it just the dumb luck__
__of a stupid, brainwashed, kid?__ There is, in fact, only one
way to find out — die and meet your maker. That was
something I wasn't looking forward to. I felt truly sorry for
all that I had done, but was this sorrow caused from my
current predicament, or was I truly remorseful? I didn't
know.

As I sat contemplating my fear and my future, the
sound of Arabic being spoken loudly changed my thoughts.
__Did they find the guy that I killed? Here I am only a few__
__feet away, trying not to make a sound. There has to be at__
__least four of them!__ I could hear one arguing and getting
louder. I guessed he was the leader and was mad at what
he'd come across. He knew someone was in the building,
but where? It was only a matter of time now. They'd narrow
down the search and there I'd be, in full view.

I needed a plan. They had every advantage if they
opened the elevator shaft. They could throw down a grenade
and that would be that. I decided, when I thought they'd
gone, I would try to open the escape door of the elevator and
drop into the elevator car, just in case. I really didn't know
what to do, but I knew I was screwed if they found me.

After about an hour of constant arguing, the group
outside left. My heart was beating so hard I thought for sure
they'd hear it, and I'm surprised they didn't. They had gone
and I hoped, this time, for good. I knew if I could hold out
for three days the Marines would be knocking on the door.
The thought was all that kept me going.

I tried the security hatch on top of the elevator which,
surprisingly, opened rather easily. I poked my head in and
looked around — nothing. I dropped into the elevator and I

closed the hatch, just in case someone had the idea to open the elevator doors and look into the shaft. All that was left to do was sit back, pray, and wait for this to end. I knew sleep was out of the question, but I wished for it. I still wrestled with the thought that this was God's way of opening my eyes and making me suffer for the choices and inexcusable actions I had taken in my life.

I needed someone to talk to, so, as stupid as it may sound, in a creative moment I named the elevator Elle. The personification of the elevator somehow made me feel better. I explained my actions to Elle in an effort to justify my life. She didn't answer. I was alone, but I kept trying. The heat was extreme and I had very little water. I knew I wouldn't last for three days with only one and half canteens of water. I was going to die, either from thirst or by gunfire. I thought about letting myself be captured, then praying that my country would rescue me, like a mother does a child in distress, but reality set in. I knew what was going to happen. I would be tortured unmercifully and killed. Why not face facts? I figured, if it came down to it, we'd shoot it out, I'd take some of them with me and then face God for my actions. I had a day to think about it. I remembered a quote from Shakespeare: "Cowards die many times before their deaths. The valiant never taste of death but once." How was it going to be with me? I was already facing cowardice, and I didn't like it. I was going to die honorably, and the only ones who would know were God and the Iraqis.

I tried to understand what fear was, and why I was so scared now and never at any other time in my life, except perhaps in Honduras. Maybe because death seemed at hand and it was just me and Elle. I took out my knife and carved Elle into a wooden panel in the elevator. Now she had her name. I asked her aloud, "Why am I was so scared?" Then it became clear. Who wouldn't be afraid, had they lived the life I had? Life is so short. You should make the most of it, and of what you believe. I thought I had. I believed in

America, what it stood for. I wished I believed in God with the same passion I had for my country. I remembered people asking, "Why do you do it? Why a sniper? Why take such a risk?" It was because of the man next to me, his family, my family, our values, and our way of life. It was that simple for me. The willingness to risk one's life for another can be a hard concept to understand, but many do it. They should be appreciated rather than judged.

I wanted someone with me so badly. I didn't want to be alone. I was hoping God would be there, help me through this time, but He was absent, or so I felt. I didn't blame Him. The only time I needed to talk to Him was when I was in trouble. In my eyes, it was too little, too late. I should have started earlier. I still could have done my missions, but with divine guidance. I had been young and invincible. I came from a country that was very diverse in its belief in God. I was confused and scared.

At that moment, I heard a noise. ***Oh, God, what is it now?*** I heard the clatter of footsteps, and they were coming from right outside of the elevator door! The footsteps fell silent and were gone. The awful sound of Arabic started again. I wished I could understand it. No one was yelling this time, just the sound of talking from where I had left the body behind. They must have been trying to decide where I might have gone. I should have left the building — gone somewhere farther away from the body, but I felt I should stay put and wait it out. ***What if it is God's will? So be it.*** The talking seemed to go on for hours, but in reality it was probably only a few moments. The sound of footsteps started going off in a different direction. It sounded like they were going to search the building. They weren't leaving until they found me. I would have done the same thing.

I sat waiting for the doors to open. They'd find their prize — they knew there was one more American. I'm sure there was quite a reward for anyone who could find me. But I reminded myself that I wasn't dealing with the brightest

157

military, and that kept me going. What were the chances they would search the building I was in, and open the door to the elevator car in which I was sitting? I hoped the chance was slim, but it wasn't out of the question.

The next few hours were the worst as I sat and waited. Scared wasn't a close description of what I felt. I wished God would ease my fears, but there was nothing. The rest of the evening I sat, not making a sound. Luck was on my side that day. The doors never opened.

Is this God's way of punishing me? The fact was, anticipation was worse than reality. There was a big part of me that actually *wanted* to be found. Let the fighting start so I could get this over with and be at peace! But I sat there, hour after hour, listening to footsteps and idle chatter. I knew one thing — if there was a Hell, I was in it. I think torture would have been better than sitting and waiting. I couldn't shake the feeling of being alone. I wondered if my friends, who had died just hours ago, were with me. I think they were. I wished countless times that I had died and they were here instead of me. Selfish! I felt guilty for them dying and me living. Why was I meant to live? Why were they meant to die? Maybe there was a reason, but I couldn't grasp it. I felt the guilt — they had died and I hadn't. I prayed to them many times that day. I prayed for their help out of that situation. I believed they were with me, that they protected me like the brotherhood we had when they had lived. Perhaps my friends were there guiding the Iraqis away from me. Hodge once told me that I had a gift for life. I thought he was full of it, but now I wasn't so sure. Damn the luck! Maybe it was a curse of life, not a gift.

A Marine is not just another soldier. He is a part of a big family. A family of a select few and a family that is proud. I took great pride in being a Marine. I was honored to die being a Marine. It's funny how such a simple title can affect the way you feel about something.

I picked up my head one more time and whispered to

myself, "You're a Marine! Toughen up! You're going to make it and tell this story! You're going to tell about loyalty, pride, integrity, courage, honesty, and honor! All the things the Marines hold sacred! You're going to live it!"

I didn't know whether other branches of the military were like this, but this was my Marine Corps perspective. I knew that the Marines were proud, and so was I. It was okay to be scared. I wasn't alone. My brothers were with me, in spirit or just around the corner, coming for my rescue. They were there. They would find me.

I looked down at my watch. It was 1830 hours. Night was coming and I would be safe for another day. As it grew later, I contemplated sneaking out to search for water and food. I considered going back to check on my friends, but was convinced the bodies would be gone. I could only imagine what the Iraqis would do their bodies. They would probably parade them through the streets showing the Kuwaitis how they conquered the Marines. The thought of my friends being dragged through the streets infuriated me. One of the most sacredly held values of the Marine brotherhood is never leaving our dead behind, but I had no choice. To stay on the rooftop meant I would have died with them. I left. It had been a matter of self-preservation. I hoped they'd forgive me. I vowed to find them once the Marines came into town.

I sat in the elevator for another couple of hours. The noise level had dropped off to complete silence. I rationalized my next move. I needed supplies. I was the best sniper in the unit. I could go out undetected, get water, and maybe with some luck, food, and return to Elle. I really had no choice. I could either stay there and die or try and survive. Camouflage and concealment were the tools of my trade. They were now going to be employed to the fullest. This wasn't school. It was real.

I climbed up to the doors, slid my knife blade into the crack, and slowly pried the doors open about two inches —

just enough to poke my little pin-like mirror out of the door check to see if the coast was clear. The coast was clear and I was mentally ready. I opened the doors just enough to get out, and then slid them back into the closed position. I slowly started for the roof to try and get some sort of surveillance of the area and check for an enemy.

Around every corner I anticipated a gun battle to begin. Then, as I made my way to a common area of the building, I saw the most delightful sight — a water dispenser! I hoped the dispenser had something like a small reserve tank inside. If the electricity had been on, all I would have had to do was fill my canteens, but no such luck. I knew there was water there somewhere, either in the pipes or in a reservoir, and I was going to find it. I took off the faceplate and could see a small container that looked like a reservoir of sorts. I loosened the connection of a small pipe that went into the bottom of the small tank. It must have been the cooling reservoir for the fountain. As I loosened the nut and slowly pulled the small tube off, I could see small droplets of water dripping by my fingers. I put the tube back up and got out both my canteens. Removing the tube, I filled my first canteen, and then replaced the tube. I gave a little test drink and then I drank a whole canteen. It was amazing how good water tasted. I refilled the canteen, replaced the water tube, and then replaced the faceplate with only a few screws, in case I needed to do this again. It would be nice to find some food, but I wasn't willing to push my luck.

I started slowly making my way back up to the top, keeping an eye out for the Iraqis or any food that may have been left behind. I finally made it to the top of the building, but couldn't find a way to get to the roof — and I needed to get to the roof. I saw the stair passage on the other side. I went over to it and slowly made my way out to the rooftop. I expected to find someone there, but my luck was holding and it was empty. Now I had the advantage of high ground. I felt alive again.

I lay down on my stomach and low-crawled around the rooftop, slowly peering over each side. I made my way to the north side and eased my head over the edge to get a glimpse of the surrounding area. I used a tactic of slowly moving my head up, looking, and slowly moving my head back down, as movement is apt to be noticed with fast and jerky movements. I made a point not to sit with my head peering over the edge. A building normally doesn't have a bump on a roof edge, and an observant individual would quickly identify a human head. I peeked over the north edge and saw a few lights and people moving around. Not a large number of personnel, just a few. I also saw a couple of cars being driven.

I moved slowly to the east side. To the east lay a large plane that had been blown in half, but there was no movement in the area. I saw more life on the west side. I was surprised to see light and people and cars moving around. My first thought was that these were Kuwaitis coming out of their houses. I began to wonder if the Iraqis were starting to pull out. Perhaps they knew we were close and coming in.

I made my way to the south end of the building. I saw what looked like a fire in a trash can and Iraqi army personnel. It looked somewhat like a lookout command post. I counted approximately six personnel. From what I could tell, they all carried weapons. Was this what was left of the Iraqis? There must be more, but where? I was glad they weren't in the building where I was currently holed up, and I felt somewhat relieved. I was going to be safe in this building, unless they decided to make it a command post. That would be a nightmare!

I decided to stay on the rooftop for another hour or two and continue observing the area. I kept a close eye on the little lookout post. I sat down by the south wall and started thinking again. I could hear noises from the streets below and wondered if, at any minute, someone would come to the rooftop and a firefight would break out. God must have been on my side that night. What would I do if the Iraqis did come to the rooftop? Surely a firefight would bring more personnel out of the woodwork. How many more were there? I knew there couldn't be that many left in the area. They appeared to have started clearing out. These were not Republican Guard, only simple, recruited soldiers of Saddam's and they knew the Marines were coming. My plan was to jam the door. If they did come up and I was there, they would leave instead of trying to knock down the door. Everything was in such a state of destruction, hopefully they would think a jammed door was just another part of it.

As I looked over the edge for the last time, I saw more personnel talking by the fire. I decided I had enough for one night and it was time to head back down to Elle. I made my way down the stairs, taking my time to check more of the building and search for food. I felt more secure knowing where the enemy was and knowing that I was safe in the building. I knew I had to be careful not to cast shadows in the windows, so I didn't walk by any of them. I either stayed in the middle of the rooms, or low-crawled around. I found one room that must have been the office of someone of importance. The furniture was exceptionally nice. I went through the desk, but found nothing. I found some magazines, took them, and kept on searching. I needed something to take my mind off my problems.

About an hour into my search, I heard voices — and they weren't coming from outside. I stopped all movement and tried to pinpoint their exact whereabouts. The voices sounded like they came from the next floor below me — the floor I needed to get to. Now I was caught, all because I needed to go exploring. Fear set back in. I was in trouble. I was in an office with nowhere to move and no place hide. If I moved too much, they'd be able to hear me. At night it seems that everything is intensified. I did what I thought was best. I crawled under the desk and sat for what seemed an eternity. ***How long are they going to be down there? Are they going to come up?*** After a couple of hours, I couldn't hear anything. I moved out to head back to Elle, hole up, and not move again. As I crawled from under the desk, I stopped to listen. Nothing. What a pleasant sound! I approached the first corner and tried to use my mirror, but it was too dark to see. I said my first real prayer in a long time and moved out.

I made my way to the stairs, and slowly opened the door. It let out a small squeak. My heart pounded again. My every sound resounded like an alarm in my imagination. I starting to think I'd have a heart attack. My heart was taking quite a bit of abuse. I stopped for a minute. I contemplated opening the elevator door from this floor and sliding down the cables, rather than attempting to make it down to the next floor. The thought passed as quickly as it came and down the stairs I went. Reaching the next floor, I'd planned to slip out and get to Elle, but something stopped me from opening the door. Call it Divine Intervention, but I wasn't supposed to go through that door.

I made my way back to the upper floor, opened the squeaky door very slowly and went to the elevator shaft door. I took my knife and slowly pried open the door just enough to stick my head in and look down on Elle. The car looked like it was 100 feet below me, but in actuality it was only 30 to 40 feet. I decided that sliding down the cables was the only way I could get down to her safely. I opened the doors a little more, slipped inside, and positioned my feet in a way that I wouldn't fall to certain death. I held on tight to the cable, placed my foot on the edge, then closed the doors as quietly as possible. With that task accomplished, I started making my way down to Elle. I wrapped part of my cammies on the cable to avoid getting metal slivers in my hands, and slowly began making my way down. After dropping down one floor, my hands were getting hot from sliding on the cable. I stopped, pushed my feet against the edge, gave myself a little rest, and listened. I didn't hear anything, so, down I went. I was now almost to Elle, when something caught my attention. Sound — the sound of snoring! I slowly stepped onto Elle and sat in silence, listening. I couldn't believe this was happening. What luck! Someone sleeping in the building! They must have come in when I was up on the roof and decided to camp out for night. I didn't think anyone had been positioned there to see if they could locate me. I knew the Iraqis knew I was still there in the area. Now what? If I were to go out and kill this guy, they'd surely be on me tomorrow. From what I could tell, this sounded like only one person. I could take him out silently, but instinct told me to stay put and be quiet.

After sitting awhile, I remembered not wanting to go through the stairway door. I called it Divine Intervention and that's what it was. At times, you get feelings. This time it paid off. I don't know what would have happened had I opened the door. We probably would have shot it out, signaling the rest to come join the battle. That was all in the past. Now I was sitting here listening to someone just outside snoring as he waited for me to appear so he could claim his prize. I knew tonight sleep was out of the question. I imagined going to sleep, starting to snore and him waking up to hear me. Not a chance!

I sat with my confiscated magazines, unable to look at them for fear of making a sound. I put them down and sat thinking of what could be next. Why weren't the Marines there yet? Perhaps since they hadn't heard from us, they'd assume that we'd been killed. When Somali and Moon-pie were hit with the RPG, so was the radio. As far as anyone knew we were all dead and they were coming into Kuwait City blind, unless there had been another recon team, which I doubted.

I kept my ears trained on everything happening outside. I didn't want anything else to catch me by surprise.

For hours I sat. At times I heard the Iraqi, at times it was quiet. I started to think about how lucky I had been so far. I'd been able to evade them, through everything. I had come so close to being caught, yet hadn't been. Why? Were my friends living up to their oaths as Marines, even in death? Was it God? Was there something else in store for me? I hoped it was a little of both. One thing was certain; the religious aspects of my life had gone from nil to praying 20 times a day. I hoped that if I prayed enough, if God didn't have time to hear the first he'd at least catch the others.

I started thinking about the end of my days. What could I expect were I to die? Would it be Heaven or Hell? I was sure I was on a straight path to Hell, but that wasn't what I wished for. I wanted a plan to make it to Heaven; but how? I remembered reading the Bible. When Jesus was on the cross, one of the two thieves asked Jesus to remember him in Heaven. He hadn't asked for absolution of his earthly sins, only to be remembered by Christ. He had taken full responsibility for the evil he'd wrought and hadn't attempted to avoid punishment. The end result was he'd been forgiven and allowed entry into Heaven. I came to realize that salvation was only granted though true remorse, not from some barter because one might find himself in dire straits. I started to talk to God again, attempting to explain my life, though I wasn't sure He'd understand. I told Him if I made it out alive, I would do His work to the best of my ability. I asked how I would know if He spoke to me. Like a whisper, I heard it.

"Listen to your feelings and act upon them."

I knew, right then, God was pointing me in the right direction. Whether or not it was true was a matter of faith, but it comforted me.

As I was sitting there contemplating my life with God, I heard the Iraqi outside get up and start moving around. I heard what sounded like the man urinating on the wall. *Great! Now I get to sit here and smell piss for two*

more days! Listening to him made me have to go. This was not my day. If he sat back down, there was no way I could go. He would surely hear me. I sat there and held it. To my surprise, it sounded like he was leaving, maybe going back down to the command post. I gave it a good 10 minutes of silence and then let it go down the side of Elle. What a relief. I sat back down and tried get a little sleep. I rested my head on my gas mask and took off into a deep sleep for what seemed like days.

Chapter 13
Remembering Life – Kuwait City Airport, Day 2

I woke feeling well and, at first, hoping that this nightmare was only just a dream. Unfortunately, reality set in. I looked down at my gas mask, at Elle's walls, and realized that the nightmare was very real. I checked my watch. It was 0500 hours. I was hungry. So close to death and all I could think about was a cheeseburger. How good would that taste? I was starving. I broke into the remainder of my MRE and ate breakfast. It was called "dehydrated pork patties," and it tasted awful. But this was no time to be a finicky eater. A few days without food and anything looked good.

It seemed quiet out in the hall. I had a look at the magazines for a little while. The first one resembled Time. It had lots of different kinds of pictures, which was good since I couldn't read Arabic. One of the pictures reminded me of school back in Montana. I'd seen the picture back at Mary Ennis Kindergarten, my first school. The thoughts of past times flooded back to me. I remembered playing Red Rover. How simple life had been. No bills, no responsibility, no thoughts of guilt. My teacher had been the greatest. She was so nice. She'd given me milk and a towel to take a nap on. I wished I could go back and try it all again.

I wondered how many people sat back and looked at their lives and said, "If I could only go back and change just one thing..." Now I was one of those people. What would I have done differently? I knew I would have tried harder in high school and I'd have gone to college. I never really liked school, but now, looking back, I realized how important it was. Had I gone to school, would I still have joined the

Marines? Would I be here, not as an enlisted man, but as an officer? I would have loved to lead troops into battle. What else would I have changed? Hopefully, I would have given my choices a lot more thought rather than acting on the spur of the moment. Maybe I'd have listened to my elders more, instead of thinking of them as less informed. Not that it mattered. I'd been young and thought I knew everything. I realized then that I knew nothing.

Thumbing through the magazine, I noticed a picture of two children playing with a goat. It reminded me of home and two of my childhood friends, Chad and Brian. I'd envied them so much. They had a great family, a ranch, cows, and horses; everything I'd always wanted. We were good friends. They were always there if I needed them and I tried to reciprocate. Some of the best times I had were with the two brothers. I remember playing at night, running through neighbors' yards and terrorizing the neighborhood. We'd once run through an old lady's garden. She'd come out, caught us, and started chewing our butts. She knew Chad and Brian, but didn't know me. I started laughing immediately. Every time I got into trouble I started to laugh. The woman was mad and it didn't help once I started laughing. The brothers got it from their old man, but I escaped any deserved punishment. The brothers would have parties out on the ranch. The fun we'd had! I sat looking at the pictures, remembering being a kid and loving life.

Other pictures reminded me of the horrors of death. A picture of starving people ended my trip into my happy memories. Death was always present. There was no getting around it. I started wondering about God again. Why would such a loving God allow this misfortune? I wished for a Pastor. There were many questions about life and God. Would your suffering in this world reward you with a higher place in the next?

I turned the pages and found pictures of food. If God were punishing me, it was working. The picture was of someone cooking what looked like beef. Probably a camel, but no matter, it looked good and all I could think about was food. I remembered poaching deer and elk for my brother, mother, and I to eat. We'd swipe potatoes from the potato factory and have a feast. Those were the times I remembered being the happiest. We'd been poor, but we made the most out of what we had. I wondered if those I saw living in poverty in the magazine were happy. Life wasn't always about money. It was about being together; spending time with family and enjoying their company.

I must have been losing it. Leafing through the magazine, I stood up, told God get me through this, and started doing a little dance. I sat back down and wondered if I'd finally lost my mind. Who in their right mind would just stand up and dance while looking death in the eye? At the very back of the magazine was a picture of a boy and mother listening to a radio. It brought back memories of my mom and me watching horror movies as kid. I'd get scared and she'd allow me to sleep by her bed at night. Sometimes she would reach down and grab me. I'd let out a scream and she would get the giggles.

The reminiscing was brought to a halt by the sound of footsteps. I immediately put down the magazine and grabbed my weapon. This was it! They were coming back, and this time they'd find me hiding in an elevator shaft like a coward. Fear was quickly exiting my mind. The thought of getting caught was more plausible. I didn't care anymore. Let them come and let's finish this. I could hear the voices again. This time they were right above me at the doors I'd opened to get into Elle. *Did I leave some sort of trail leading here? Had I forgotten something? Were the doors closed? Why had they come straight here?* I was in a bad position for a firefight. I thought about starting to scream. *That'd get this over with!* I lay on my back, rifle at the ready, and watched for the doors to open.

I could hear them talking. I heard what I thought

were the doors being opened, but it must have only been one of them leaning against the doors. I said what I thought to be my last prayer. *God, give me one more day, please! I want so badly to go home; to be with my family again! There are so many things left in this life to accomplish! I need to right so many people that I've wronged!* I told myself if I made it out, I'd never kill another living thing. I needed to make things right in my life. *God, give me a chance to prove that I've changed; that I understand life and what it means to be a human being!*

I tried to think of what to do if the doors did indeed open. I was still operating in self-preservation mode. Even if it meant killing more Iraqis, I couldn't let them take me like a coward. I was trying to make peace with God. I hoped he'd understand these people were a work of the Devil. He'd seen the atrocities these people had inflicted. I felt I'd made my peace. I was going to start working for the other side, but needed a chance to prove it. That meant getting out of this jam and living the change I felt.

I heard screaming and what sounded like a fight breaking out. There was a lot of noise, and then the awful sound of gunfire — a single shot and I was sure a single kill. I knew the sound of gunfire would attract more people. More Iraqis were about to show up and whatever was about to happen was sure to start happening soon.

The possibilities started rolling through my mind. *What happens if the shooter leaves, and didn't tell the truth? The others will surely think that I am still here and am killing their personnel. This is great! One more day and something like this happens! Couldn't I have a quiet day? On the other hand, maybe it was a fight over leaving and giving up on me...*

The last scenario was the one I liked best, but I was sure my first thoughts would be more likely. I sat and waited. The Iraqi shooter was going to blame me for the killing and the search for me would be on. I heard someone leaving and

170

a door slamming. This guy was in trouble and wanted to place the blame on me quickly before anyone started to question his story. Now I had a decision to make. Should I go to the roof and try and fight it out there? Should I stay put? I weighed my options. If I went to the roof, I'd have a fighting chance. I could kill more of them and maybe save my own neck; however, they were sure to find me up there. Sitting there on top of Elle I wasn't in the best fighting position, but I was well hidden. Yet, if a firefight broke out, I would most certainly die.

I decided to stay put and ride it out. I knew it was coming. I thought about the elevator's doors. They really couldn't be opened because they were between floors. I looked toward the top of the elevator shaft and something caught my eye. It looked like a little crawl space at the top where they did maintenance. From what I could tell, it looked to be two or three feet wide on both sides in the wall. It was hard to tell because of the poor lighting in the shaft. There was only one way to be sure. I had to climb my way up four flights of cable. The good outweighed the bad, so I packed up all my belongings, making sure not leave anything behind. If they found something on top of the elevator, they would definitely know I had been there.

I started my way to the top. Foot by painful foot I climbed up the cable. Thank God I was in good shape. It helped that I could push against the doors and rest at each floor. It wasn't an easy climb, but if I did make it to the top and that was a cubbyhole, I'd have a better chance of hiding and more of a chance of fighting. At least they wouldn't be able to toss a grenade in on me, and I would have the advantage of high ground.

I finally made it to the top. What I thought was a three-foot cubbyhole was, in fact, a little smaller. The space was more like 1 ½ feet. Once I crawled up into it, I saw a more delightful sight. I could actually get on top of the cable stabilizers on top. This was definitely where they did maintenance on the elevator. Even more surprising, there was a small door leading to the roof, or so I thought. I was about to open the door when I heard another door open. *Why are these people still here? Can't they just leave? Did I pick the wrong building or what?* I lay on the top of the maintenance shaft trying to conceal myself. This time I heard more than one person, the sound of a lot of footsteps, and several doors opening and closing. They appeared to stop where I assumed the dead Iraqi was. They talked for just a few minutes and left as fast as they'd come.

What was going on out there? I couldn't wait for nightfall so I could go out and do some investigating. It quieted down again and I again wondered where the Marines were. I started thinking of my friends who had died just a short time ago. Hodge had been my best friend. I'd gone through so much with him, and now he lay dead in this godforsaken place. The worst part was I'd left him and my other two friends to be subjected to humiliation by these people. The guilt was unbearable. How could I tell the Marines I left them to the Iraqis? Would they understand, or would I be an outcast? I should have stayed and died with them. In hindsight, that seemed the only honorable thing to do. I was going to be labeled as a coward. I didn't know any of Hodge's, Somali's, or Moon-pie's families, but I needed to tell them what happened. I wanted their families to know that each of their sons died honorably. They died saving my life. That's how I looked at it. Not just my life, but my spirit as well. I liked to think they were ready for Heaven. Was that why God choose to take them and not me? Was that why I remained to face a lifetime of their memory and my cowardice? I had always thought of myself as the meanest and bravest of my platoon, but if they only knew. My mission now was to stay alive, to keep my friends' legacies alive, and honor how they died for a country in which they believed so greatly.

My biggest regret was I never got a chance to say

goodbye, especially to Hodge. We'd been through so much. All he wanted to do was complete his commitment and become a teacher. That was all gone now. He died and I am still here with the burden. Hodge will never be forgotten. He was my friend. I'll miss him until I die. I am sorry I didn't get a chance to tell him how proud I was of him. I promised myself I'd make sure his family knew what a hero he'd been and that he changed my life forever. His death caused me to become a changed man. I thank God for Hodge every day He lets me live.

I thought about 1st Sergeant Press' story — the reaction when he'd told the truth and how his family and his friend's family had turned on him. Now I understood his actions, and why I had done the same. It wasn't quite the same — I didn't kill them, so to speak, but I might as well have. I led them into a gun battle that caused their deaths. It was my obligation to tell them. I especially wanted to talk to Hodge's parents. He'd been brave. He'd been a great friend. He'd been truly a great Marine that deserved recognition for his devotion to country and family that he loved so much.

I hadn't forgotten Somali and Moon-pie. Their families had the right to know the kind of men their sons were. Each had more pride, integrity, and loyalty than anyone I had ever met. I was privileged to know them and serve next to them. I wanted their families to know they should hold their heads high and be proud of the men their sons had become.

What do I tell my own family? How do I explain what happened here? Do I just let it die? Say nothing? I wasn't happy with the way I carried out this mission. I was sure my mother wouldn't care. It wouldn't matter what I'd done, as so long as I came home, but it mattered to me. I'd killed my friends, left their bodies, then had the audacity to hide like a coward and beg God for help. I'd never asked God for help before. I began to wonder how I'd face myself in the mirror. What about my home town? I'd spent so long trying to prove myself. Would they view me as a disgrace? I couldn't handle it anymore! I opened the trap door and went out onto the roof.

I could not live my life thinking I was a coward. If I died, maybe no one would know the truth and I could be a brave, honorable soldier instead of a coward.

I sat at the door and counted my ammunition. I didn't have my sniper rifle, just short-range firepower. It was nice to see the daylight and even better to see no Iraqis. I sat in broad daylight, waiting for the attack to begin. I heard the sound of cars from below. I didn't investigate. I knew better than to stick my head over the side — I wasn't ready to die just yet. Now I had a way to the top of the roof and to Elle. I could move around the building in stealth. Now what to do? I could lay on the roof. Get a tan. Try to signal an American helicopter. I knew the helos would be coming again and didn't want them to mistake me for an Iraqi. I had questions, but no answers. Regardless of the demons that came and went from my thoughts, my main focus was still to try to stay alive.

Now that I was facing death, opposing thoughts went through my head. One moment I felt guilty for the death of my friends. Seconds later, I counted my blessings for being alive. I don't think my friends would have stayed and died pointlessly. I would have wanted them to leave, to save themselves and stay alive. Maybe I had done the right thing. Only time would tell. For now, I'd sit and wait. This was far from over.

I continued hearing the cars, but no gunfire. I could distinguish the sounds of people talking. Hearing the sounds of cars and people made me feel at ease. I sat and listened. I wondered how many times I'd sat and listened to life. Did I go along with my life so fast that everything passed me by? I looked at the clouds, and started to make out images. How many times had I taken for granted the miracle of sight? I promised myself that from then on I'd look at everything differently. I wished I had answers. I was a young, scared kid, trying to do what was right. Understanding right from wrong is hard enough from day to day, much less in the midst this chaos. I knew I loved my country. I knew I'd gladly do all this again. I had to believe in something. I believed in America and what her promise stood for.

For the rest of the day I sat on the rooftop, looked at my magazines, and let the cards fall where they may. From time to time I thought about my family and friends.

I fell asleep, daydreaming. I must have dozed for quite a while, because when I woke up, it was dusk. I sat and listened. I could still hear cars and people, but no gunfire. *Is it over? Did they leave?* I now went to the east, west, north and south corners and took a peek. Surprisingly, there were no Iraqis. The command post was empty. I could see people moving, but no one in uniform. I decided go down to the floor where I'd heard the shot and investigate. As I made my way down the stairs, I saw what was once a beautiful building now totally destroyed. It made me sick to think what destruction war does to humanity and the beautiful things we create.

Reaching the floor, I found a body lying in the hall just above Elle. The body appeared to have been robbed. His pockets were turned out, gun taken, and no sign of jewelry. Why?

What did you do to be shot by your own? These people really were animals. I couldn't have done this. As I looked at the face, it occurred to me how ugly war was, people turning on each other and killing their own. Unbelievable! But, another dead Iraqi was of no concern to me, so I kept searching. Down the hall the body of the man I'd killed lay rotting. I passed by and kept searching room to room, occasionally sneaking a peek to see what was happening outside. At one point, I saw civilians milling around. I wondered if any would come into this building. If they did, what was I supposed to do? Would they turn me in or greet me with open arms? I liked to think they would be glad to see Americans, but I would worry about that if one of them found me.

The day had ended and I was totally out of food. It would be nice to find something edible. I continued searching for food and as a side objective, some Intel on what was happening outside. I made my way down to the first floor and started working my way through each room. I found some more magazines and took them. I searched the rest of the area and found nothing. I headed back up, made my way back to the cubbyhole, and looked through my new reading material.

I sat down in the top of the of the elevator shaft, switched on my little blue-filter light, and leafed through the magazines. Food seemed to be on every page. I considered cutting out the pictures and eating them. I was starving, but could do without food for days. I'd done it many times in my military training. Water was the necessity. I had enough remaining for a day or two. I might have to go back down to the fountain to refill my canteens, but I didn't want to think about that now. I flipped a page and there was a picture of a child playing in water. One of my fondest childhood memories was of playing in a friend's pond. The picture was a reminder; not only of the pond back home, but that I stunk and needed shower. If the Iraqis couldn't hear me, they should have been able to smell me by now. On the next page was another picture of war. As a bonus, the photographer had managed to capture images of starving people in the photo — more of man's inhumanity to man. Every magazine seemed to contain a reminder of war, hunger, and destruction. I was tired of it. I wanted to focus on the good, but the ugly seemed to sell. Was death and destruction all we wanted to see? Did we have to focus on all life's wrongs?

Dawn was breaking. The night was coming to an end, and for some reason, I felt I was too. Throughout the day all

176

I'd done was recall my childhood memories. In a way, I was glad no one had come and I'd had the day to myself. It had brought a change into my life and many fond memories.

I set my gas mask down on a cable hoist, propped my head on it, and lay down to sleep. As I drifted off, the memories continued to come. I was finally at peace. I talked to God once more. I thanked Him for giving me these last couple of days to grow and learn to ask for forgiveness. I had no doubt this time. I knew I was truly sorry for not having God in my life. From that day forward I would rely on God's guidance. I would try and work in his ways through this strange and wonderful life. I fell fast asleep, into a wonderful world of dreams.

Chapter 14
Embracing Death – Kuwait City Airport, Day 3

I woke up with the same sense of peace. I hoped the Marines would make it in, but I was also okay if they didn't. I'd never felt this way before. I was ready for death or rescue. Or should I say...recovery. In my eyes, God had already provided rescue. I was 10 feet tall. I had God by my side. There was no more time for guilt or fear. I was cared for. The poem "Footprints" was now, more than ever, in my mind. God was carrying me through the hard times.

It was time to try and get out of there and find my brothers. I looked down at my watch. It was 0520. I knew the Marines were knocking on the door. It was time to find them. I opened the trap door and made my way to the roof.

Once on the roof, I looked around and found nothing unusual. It was all right now. I wasn't afraid to die anymore. It was a great feeling. I looked around each side of the building, not caring if I was seen or not. I knew I could hold the Iraqis off, at least for the day. My brothers were coming. God was with me. Who could possibly be scared? I decided not to stay on the roof. If the helos showed up, I didn't want to be mistaken for an Iraqi sniper. The best place for me was inside, sitting on top of Elle and waiting for help to come. I could come to the roof periodically to get an idea of when the Marines would be coming.

I made my way back down to my cubbyhole. I laid out all my magazines and put my weapon down, and made myself a little nest. The Marines were coming today. They were scheduled to do so, and I didn't have any doubt they'd make it. I was still nervous about what they'd think of me for leaving my friends. I hoped they'd understand. I had had no choice except to stay and die. I prayed I'd made the right decision. I sat for what seemed like hours, when a noise I knew so well came to my ears — the sound of helicopters flying overhead. I immediately grabbed my things and headed for the roof. I slowly opened the door and took a peek out. To my relief, I could see Marine Cobras and Army Apaches overhead. I kept my cool and stayed inside the door. If the helos were there, the Marines would be close by. My instinct told me not to go out, so I stayed put and watched joyous sight of the U.S. helos filling the Kuwaiti sky. I heard the sound of vehicles. Not cars, but military vehicles. They were there and they were coming in by the hundreds. It was only a matter of time before I was safe.

I waited in my cubbyhole. I sat there, heart pounding, and wondered what I would be facing. The longer I waited, the more I was convinced I wouldn't face charges. There had been around 40 Iraqis starting to surround the building we'd been in. I was as good as dead had I not made my escape. If any of my friends had been alive, I'd have stayed until the end, but it hadn't worked out that way. Staying would have only prolonged the inevitable — the humiliation of having the bodies dragged through the streets. The only difference was I'd have been dragged with them. I'd tell the truth and let the cards fall where they may. The Marines could do no worse to me than I'd done to myself these last few days. I was tired of thinking about it. I just wanted it to be over.

I decided to wait until I could hear English being spoken. To kill time, I broke out my magazines again and started looking at pictures. I didn't have to wait long. I began to hear sporadic gunfire. The Marines must have found the Iraqis. What to do now — head to the roof, or sit here and wait? I started making my way to the roof when I heard personnel coming in and slamming doors. By the sound and commotion, it could have been by the hundreds. Were these the Marines, or Iraqis coming to set up for a final battle in what was left of the airport hotel? I pressed my ear as close as possible to the wall and listened. If these were Iraqis setting up an ambush for the Marines, they were in for a rude surprise. I was coming out and killing everything in sight. I was still set up for close-range fire and that was my game plan. I had had enough. I switched my safety off and reached for the trap door. I opened the door and listened. There was lots of noise, but no sound of English being spoken. What if the Marines weren't here yet? Was this a large group of Iraqis? The U.S. helicopters were outside, so technically I wasn't alone. I could make a stand at the top of the roof, as long as the helos didn't shoot me. That's what I was going to do.

I went through the trapdoor and started heading to the top when I heard the beautiful sound of English. They were there, coming fast and clearing the building. I continued toward the roof so I wouldn't be shot by mistake. I figured if the helo pilots knew Marines were on the ground and I looked like one of them, they wouldn't mistake me for the enemy and I'd be safe. I opened the roof door, stood up proudly, and walked straight over to the edge, looking down on the activity below. Reaching the east side, I was amazed at the number of U.S. military vehicles. I was rescued for sure! A helo flew over and I gave them a quick wave. As they circled around, my heart started pumping normally again. The big Cobra came within about 100 feet of the building and gave me a sign of acknowledgment, then went on his way. I hoped he called in, and let the troops below know I was there. Now my mission was to find the bodies of my friends as soon as possible. I prayed the Iraqis hadn't taken them.

The Marine infantry was entering the building. They had no idea I was there or what I was doing. My mission had been classified to all personnel except to the commanders. I had to find my friends, make my way to the command post, and turn myself in. I wouldn't go in for interrogation until I found out about my friends. I'd been through interrogation. I knew how the game was played. If I went in first, I'd never learn anything further of Hodge, Somali, and Moon-pie. I heard the sound of the door opening and weapons at the ready. The Marines were on the roof! I turned, saw one, held my weapon up and said, "It's clear up here." They stared at me, wondering how I'd beaten them to the top.

A sergeant came over to me. "Sergeant, what are you doin' up here and where did you come from?"

"I'm a Recon Sniper. I came in two days earlier."

"You probably need to go down and talk to my commanding officer."

"I only answer to my commander. Anything I have to say is classified. This wasn't a regular operation. Where is your command post and where is the main command post? I needed to see Colonel Jack."

"I'm not sure I know who that is. We've made most of the command post down on the airfield. This is Task Force Ripper that came in. I'm not sure about anyone else."

The sergeant had a two-squad element with him, nine personnel total. He called in on the radio and started to talk to someone on the other end. He told them about me. I look at him and said, "Sergeant, I have to go."

"Wait a minute."

I ran past his troops. To hell with this — I needed answers, not questions. I ran down the stairs headed for the first floor as the personnel stood staring at me. *How am I going to get out of this mess?* I needed to get back to my friends. I didn't need this right now. Running toward the end of the building, I heard several Marines shouting for me to halt. I knew the sergeant at the top of the building had called in on me and they were waiting on me to come out of the building. They weren't going to shoot me. I kept running. I could hear several Marines running behind me. I didn't bother to look back. I kept running for the building where my friends lay dead, and nothing was going to stop me. I kept hearing them behind me, "Stop! Marine, stop!" I kept running until one of them grabbed a hold of my back. I stopped, turned and started to chew some ass. Turning around, I noticed about 10 Marines right behind him. This was a Staff Sergeant and he out ranked me.

"I have to find my friends — the rest of my squad. You can come, but don't try to stop me!"

I think he knew the gravity of the situation by looking into my eyes.

"We'll go." Turning to his command, he barked a quick order. "Follow us! Sergeant, lead off."

I started jogging toward the building where I'd left Hodge. I reached the steps to the building, dreading the ascent. I stopped, looked back at the Marines, and said, "Please, just hang back for a few minutes and then come up."

The Staff Sergeant gave me the okay and I headed up.

When I reached the final step leading to the top of the building I prayed I'd find Hodge still there. I could hear his voice — "Where have you been? I'm hungry as hell!"

I pushed the door open and looked at the spot where Hodge and I were only a few days ago. What I saw was as relieving as it was dreadful. Hodge lay almost in the same spot where I'd left him. His ammo and weapons were taken and he had been robbed, but his body was intact. As I stood there looking at my friend, I must have still been in shock.

The Staff Sergeant tapped me on my shoulder and asked, "What happened here, Sergeant?"

"This is where my friends gave their lives for me. I have to check another building."

I started toward the stairs. The Staff Sergeant ordered his second squad, "Go get a body bag for this Marine."

I told him thanks and to bring two more. I made my way over to the other building to see what might remain of Somali and Moon-pie. Approaching the top I had the same haunting thought that they weren't dead and I had left them. But I had seen the small arms rocket hit them and there was no possible way they could have survived. I paused at a door.

The Staff Sergeant tapped me on the shoulder. "Is everything all right?"

"My other two friends are through this door. I don't want to go through it."

"Do you want me to go in for you?"

"They were my responsibility. I'll go."

I went through the door.

I hadn't wanted to see this. I saw my friends — or what seemed to be them. There were body parts all over the building top. I made my way over to their position. There were no weapons, only their mutilated bodies. It was hard for me to believe these were my friends. I looked back at the Staff Sergeant.

"I think I'll go have a mental check for a little while."

He asked me again, "What happened?"

I replied the same as before, "They died saving my life."

I started to leave, but the Staff Sergeant stopped me again. "You need to go back and talk to my commanding officer."

I looked at him and laughed. "I'm going back to my unit. That's where I'll talk."

He wasn't happy with my answer but I didn't care. Rank had no meaning for me at that moment.

"Would you have your guys to help clean this up? I need your unit and name. I have to give the authorities that info when I get back."

He took out a piece of paper and wrote everything down and told me that he was sorry. I touched him on his shoulder and said, "Thanks."

As I was headed toward the door, he ordered his men to move aside and let me pass. I gave him a look of thanks and headed out to find my platoon and give my report. I stepped outside and looked around to see Marines everywhere. It was a great sight. Now I faced the hard part — going back to my platoon and telling the story.

As I walked toward the command post, a young Lance Corporal stopped me. "Sergeant? You all right?"

"Why?"

"You're covered in blood."

I looked down and saw Hodge's dried blood covering my uniform. I'd become accustomed to the sight of it.

"It's okay, Corporal. It's not mine."

He stared at though in a state of shock. I turned and continued toward the command post to find 1st Sergeant Press, the one man I was not looking forward to seeing.

Several command posts were being assembled as I walked down the road. I stopped several Marines, asking them if they knew the location of my outfit, but got the same answer. "No."

I found a big circle of vehicles. Thinking this was it, I proceeded to the center where the Marines where hanging out. There were at least a hundred of them doing odd jobs around the area. I looked for the highest-ranking officer, a Light Colonel, and stopped him.

"Sir, do you know where I can find the 1st Recon Battalion 1st Sergeant or Colonel?"

"They should be somewhere over there," he replied, pointing off in distance.

I looked in the direction he pointed and headed out, wondering what to expect. It didn't matter anymore what they thought. I'd done my best. That was all that mattered. I made my way through the vehicles, getting eyed by everyone. Was I being paranoid, or did I really look *that* bad? Whatever the reason, I didn't care.

I found our vehicle but no one was inside. ***Great! Here I am and no one to tell what happened.*** I'm sure they thought we were dead and in a way, I guess we all were.

Only a short time ago, I'd been starving. Now I couldn't have eaten if I was forced. I was more nervous than I thought I'd be. I sat down and wondered what to do next. I loaded up on some ammo that I found in the Hummer, grabbed an MRE, and headed out to look for what was left of my platoon. I must have feared running into another company sized element, because I could hardly walk for the weight of the ammunition I'd loaded on me.

As I walked, I ate a few crackers and looked for my unit. I could have stayed put, but I needed to find them and get this off my chest. I was ready for interrogation. I made my way through the vehicles, looking at everyone I passed. I needed to find my 1st Sergeant and my platoon. I needed to feel at home again with my unit, my family. I needed to talk with them and get this off my chest. The stress finally caught up with me. I sat down, practically collapsing. At that instant, I realized what I had been through — the loss of my friends, the guilt of leaving them, and for the most part, the entire mission being a failure. Failure was not in the Marine vocabulary, so it wasn't in mine, but I *had,* in fact, failed. It was a bitter pill. I struggled to my feet and continued to walk and look for my unit, the whole time being stared at by the Marines I passed. I'd been to a war. They had yet to go. I should have cleaned up and changed clothes, but I had to move on.

Chapter 15

Unstable

For the first time in my life I felt weak. I was tired, hungry, unsure, unaware, dizzy, and scared. What was wrong with me? I knew I needed to find my unit, but all I could do was sit with my head on my knees and think. I was uncertain how my fellow Marines would perceive my actions and conduct. It was the one thing that bothered me most. I believed I done the best that I could — there was no way I could have fought off the enemy from my position. The odds had been overwhelming, that fact was clear — but should I have stayed? Should I have died next to my friends?

As I pondered my situation, I heard that awful voice. 1st Sergeant Press was yelling at someone. I looked up and could see Marines moving around, but that voice could only be one man. I lifted myself off the ground and started over. A death row inmate making his way to the chair couldn't have felt worse. I didn't know what to think. I'd committed a cardinal sin. I'd left a Marine behind.

I ran into one of my buddies from the platoon. He started yelling, grabbed me and hugged me. "We thought you were all dead!"

"I'm all that's left."

I saw his eyes go from excitement to sorrow. Then he took a good look at me and my uniform and said, "God! What happened?"

"I better go see 1st Sergeant Press, first. I'll tell you later."

"I'll escort you over."

It was nice to see a friendly face.

As I approached, 1st Sergeant Press was yelling at everyone and everything in sight. In an instant he looked over and saw me. He stopped in mid-sentence and gave me that look of his — but this time, the look was hard to judge. From his gaze, I thought he was expecting to see the rest of us. He paused, looked straight at me and said, "Glad to see you, Sergeant, come with me. Let's have a debrief meeting with the CO."

I slowly walked over to him. He put his arm on my shoulder and said, "Remember, you're a Marine! Marines are tough. We can get through anything, even when you think you can't. You'll get through it, time heals, and alcohol helps."

That was my pep talk. I respected this man. It helped. He blabbed on a few more positives, but he still didn't know what happened. He might change his mind after my testimony.

My CO looked at me like he'd seen a ghost. He wasn't quite as astute as 1st Sergeant Press. "Where are the others?"

"They died."

"1st Sergeant Press, go get my platoon leader and platoon Sergeant. Let's get this man debriefed, ASAP!"

I was seated in front of a Colonel with three other commanding officers, my Lieutenant, 1st Sergeant Press, and my Platoon Sergeant. I described everything; the jump in, the woman in the bunker, the firefight, the deaths of my friends, why I hadn't radioed back with Intel, my escape, the little girl in the airport, the man I killed, and finally, the three days I remained in hiding. They all stared at me. When I finished, they asked a few questions, but nothing specific. My report had been very detailed. It was 1st Sergeant Press' question that surprised me. I couldn't decide if he knew what was going through my mind or if he was psychic.

He asked, "Sergeant, how do you feel about leaving your squad behind?"

I choked up. "For three days that question burned at me. I've never felt so guilty in my life. If I had to do it over,

I'd stay to the end." I didn't know what else to say, but added, "What I did was wrong, but my friends were dead. The only way I could finish my mission was to try and stay alive."

1st Sgt. stood up and walked over to me. The others remained in their seats. "Sergeant, you have nothing to feel guilty about. You made the right decision. If it wasn't for your bravery and ability to stay alive, we would not have the Intel that you are providing us now. *That's* your job, not packing your dead friends out on your back."

I knew he was referring to his own experience. He turned, faced the other officers, and said, "This Marine needs to get back out, continue clearing buildings and finish up this war so we can all get the hell out of here."

The Colonel stood up. "Sergeant, you've done a great job and we are grateful. You should be proud. We are all sorry for the loss of our fellow Marines, but that is the nature of war. It is our vocation. We must move on."

When I left the tent, 1st Sgt. Press was right beside me. "Sergeant, when all this shit is over, we'll have a drink. Get all this out in the open and be done with it."

"Thank you, sir. I appreciate the support."

"Head back to platoon Sergeant. Go out and continue on. It gets easier, son. Friends become more like acquaintances."

Maybe he was right. Friends and war weren't compatible. It would have been easier to deal with the death of an acquaintance. My squad had been my friends. They died and some of me died with them. I couldn't finish my mission because of my impaired mental condition. Maybe that's how the old war veteran made it through so many tours in Vietnam, although I questioned 1st Sergeants Press' sanity at times.

I made my way back to the tent. I sat for a while. I ate and talked with the men in my platoon. I told and retold my story to the rest of the guys. After a couple of hours, the

Platoon Sergeant came by, told us to gather up and get ready for building clearing. I took out my M-4, loaded down with ammo, and told the squad to move out. The 1st Sergeant knew I needed to get back out. He knew it would help my mental condition. In his own way, he was an intelligent man.

Our mission was to clear each building, room to room, and take prisoners. We set parameters on several buildings and then started to clear. This was good. The activity kept my mind occupied for a while, giving me something to do besides think. The four of us went into the first floor while the others watched the exits for anyone that might be attempting to come in behind us. After clearing the first building, there was no visible sign of any Iraqis. I relaxed and wasn't alert. I wanted to go get some sleep and rest for the night. The plan was not to clear any buildings in the dark. We were to stand guard at night — buildings would only be cleared during daylight hours. The last building for the day was a small four-story. It was the place where I received a reality check.

I didn't hear one gunshot that day. It was safe to say the Iraqis were gone. My guard was down. I was so mentally drained I could barely walk up a flight of stairs. I started walking into every room with my weapon hanging at my side instead of at the ready position. My negligence was rewarded by walking in on a lone Iraqi. He had his bayonet fixed on his AK-47. As I entered the room, he hit me in the stomach several times before I realized I was being attacked. Swinging up my M-4, I pulled the trigger, emptying 30 rounds into his chest and face. The sound of gunfire brought the rest of the squad running. I stood there with the rest of the squad, staring.

"Sergeant, why'd you shoot this guy so many times?"

"I guess my magazine ran out."

I hadn't realized, in the moment, that I'd switched the selector to the full auto setting.

As we stood looking at the dead Iraqi, one of my squad said, "Good thing you were on your guard. You coulda been shot."

That's when I realized I'd been stabbed. In all the commotion I hadn't noticed. "I need to go back down and see the medic."

"Why?"

"Look! Look at me!"

Once they realized I had been stabbed, they all wanted to help me get to the medic. I told them to go ahead and finish the building. I could find my way back. I was forced to admit to myself that my relaxed behavior almost got me killed.

The squad had to have a look at my wound. A couple made petty jokes. One reached into his medical pouch saying, "Are you kidding me? You're going to the medic over that?" Then he handed me a Band-aid. We stood for a while longer talking about what to do with the Iraqi.

I finally told them, "I've gotta go to the medic. I'm bleeding all over my uniform."

Two of them escorted me down to the medic.

When I reached the medic and explained what had happened, they rushed me on a helicopter out to a Naval hospital ship for surgery. Once on board, I was dosed with morphine. I woke the next day with a drug hangover, not knowing what had happened. The surgeon came in, explained everything to me, and told me to rest. Five days later, I was packed up and ready to go home. But first I wanted to see my unit, and insisted that I go back. A call was placed to my CO and he granted me the day to see my unit one last time before leaving. He owed me that.

I boarded a helicopter for a quiet ride back to my unit. The medics wanted me in a wheelchair, but I wouldn't have any part of it. The sympathy would have been nice, but I didn't expect any. My buddies would have dogged me for eternity if I came back being pushed in a wheelchair, so I

190

walked.

When I made it back to the unit, 1st Sergeant Press approached me. "How are you, Sergeant?"

"I've got a stomach ache. You have any Tums?"

It was the first time I ever heard him laugh. I might have been the only person who had heard him laugh in 20 years. It made me feel good. He tapped me on my back and said, "Welcome to the club. Ya know, gettin' stabbed was worse than getting shot."

He would know. I enjoyed talking to him; having his attention. I felt 1st Sergeant Press had started to like me. He seemed to enjoy talking to me — not so much as a Marine, but like a son. A son he never had.

We made our way around the unit. The CO came over. "Sergeant, if you needed to go home, just ask."

I replied, "Make sure they get my name right on the medal, sir."

He smiled and answered, "They don't give medals for you doing your job. Carry on."

I sat around for the rest of the day, packing up my belongings and saying my goodbyes. Then I made it back over to the 1st Sergeant. "Sir, I have to leave. I don't think they'll let me stay with my unit until they leave."

"No. It's time to go home."

I had less than three months left in the Corps. All I could think about was staying with my unit until the end of the war. Our mission wasn't finished. I wasn't holding up my end of the bargain.

I arrived home, along with several hundred other Marines, to a hero's welcome. I didn't feel like a hero. I felt dumb allowing myself to be stabbed and guilty for having to leave my unit. Upon arrival, I was escorted to the hospital for a two-day stay. Afterward, I made it back to the barracks and met some of the crew there. I told them what had happened in Kuwait. I didn't release any information, only the facts — who died, not how. It was basic information of the missions, mostly junk and lies. Well, that was my job.

The next month came and my unit arrived home safe and sound. Everyone was still alive. The CO informed me that if I didn't reenlist, I would be transferred to a Poag Battalion. A Poag Battalion is what we called units composed of women and desk jockeys. I was a full combat marine, mustache past the corners of my mouth, and an attitude from here to China. ***WITH WOMEN? What the hell?***

"This will help your transition into the civilian world."

Since women were not part of an infantry battalion's personnel, I'd never had to work around them. I understood the concept, but it made me nervous thinking I'd be around female Marines. I hated the idea. They were career stoppers. In other words, if accused of sexual harassment, you were busted. At the time, the sexual harassment era was in full swing. I am not saying problems didn't occur, but you hear rumors. Since I didn't plan to re-up, my unit gave me up and sent me to a Poag Battalion.

The Platoon Sergeant, a female, out-ranked me. She'd never seen combat — had never done anything, really — yet she was my boss. It irked me. The move had been right. I needed to be around women and normal activities to get my head on straight; to acclimate to life outside of recon. I'd been too isolated in my career and had forgotten about everything outside of it.

I stood in formation for inspection by the Staff Sergeant. She stood in front of me and pointed out, "Sergeant, you need to get your mustache into regulations by the end of the day."

I replied, "I'll get mine into regulations as soon as you get yours into regulations." That didn't go over well, especially with most of the platoon laughing out loud. It was disrespectful and I knew it was wrong. I just didn't want to take orders from women.

I was immediately called to her office, dressed down, and informed she was writing me up. I laughed.

"Write me up. I have less than two months left. This is why I never wanted to be in a Poag. Women can't handle men or the responsibility of the military. Their course of action is to write you up. That's not the way it's handled in the real Marine Corps."

The snide little comments didn't do anything for my case. It only made her angrier. I laughed it off. The way I saw it, I'd lost my squad, almost starved to death in a elevator, had nearly been killed, and this puke wanted to write me up... because of my mustache? Go for it.

I was hauled in front of the Battalion Commander and read the riot act for my conduct. It wasn't all too bad.

"Sergeant, you've had a wonderful career in the Marines. You've made great strides in a short time. It's unfortunate that good Marines muster out." His tone was pleasant. He continued, "Sergeant, you can reenlist. We'll make you a Staff Sergeant and you can go back to old your platoon, or you can muster out as a Corporal."

"Sir, I've had enough. I need some time to get my life back in order. I'm grateful for your leniency if I choose to stay in. I know I was wrong and should be punished for my behavior toward a higher ranking NCO. I accept that. I'll move on and continue to be proactive in the last few weeks that I have left."

The CO looked at me, gave me a nod of approval, and said, "With great regret, I am removing your stripe from a Sergeant to Corporal."

I took my reduction in rank, did an about-face and walked out of the room.

The next day I stood in line with my mustache in regulations and waited for the Staff Sergeant to make her daily rounds. She walked by me and never even looked. At that moment, I realized what a jerk I'd become. I had embarrassed this NCO in front of her platoon. It wasn't appropriate behavior. I knew what I needed to do. I'd heard comments that she was wrong; what they'd done to me was out of line. For the most part, everyone in the platoon was on my side. She was losing respect and control because of my behavior.

I stepped forward and asked Staff Sergeant if I could address the platoon. You could have heard a pin drop. She granted permission, and held her breath. I asked the platoon to stand at ease. I told them some of the events of Desert Storm. I told them why I was assigned to this platoon.

"It's obvious that I need help with my social skills. What I did to the Staff Sergeant was wrong. Losing my rank because of my mouth was appropriate. The rest of you will take note and realize that respect is a Marine cornerstone. We must, at all times, keep it high on our list. I'd forgotten that. I apologize to the Staff Sergeant for my insubordination. The Staff Sergeant was doing her job. I wasn't doing mine. For the remainder of my time with this platoon, it will be an honor to remain one of the Staff Sergeant's squad leaders."

I went on for a while until I'd made myself perfectly clear. As I looked over to the Sergeant, I could see that she was grateful and accepted my apology. Later in the day, we sat down and joked a little. You might say we became friends. I finished out my time, following her orders to the letter.

The last week she came up to me and said, "I won't tell anyone if you start re-growing your mustache."

So I did. When I left, I hugged her goodbye. I'd been wrong. I'd learned a lesson. The women of the military gave as much as I, only in different ways. I hoped I'd be forgiven for having been too narrow-minded to appreciate them at the time.

Chapter 16
At the End

I mustered out of the Marines and suddenly became a civilian. For the most part, I tried to move on with my life and assimilate into society — easier said than done. Like many ex-military, I became a police officer for a little while. Still struggling with the events in Kuwait, I blamed myself for the deaths of my friends. After about a year, I was still having trouble putting the events of war in perspective. I need help, not just with the loss of my friends, but adapting with society, its rules and regulations.

God was never a part of my life before. In the past, I'd blamed my life without a father on Him. I guess I needed to blame someone. I blamed God. I blamed society. After Kuwait, God had been in my life. I was sustained through the incident in Kuwait City by that belief.

During my time as a police officer, I considered taking my own life. I wasn't doing well. I couldn't forgive myself for my friends' deaths. I decided my life was over. I would perform martial arts Katas in a deserted place where I could be alone and listen to soft music. It was peaceful and relaxing. This would be my place of death. I felt relaxed and safe there.

After planning my death, I sat on the ground, tears streaming from my eyes, begging God to forgive me what I was about to do. I told God life was too difficult. I was taking the coward's way out. It bothered me — I'd wanted to die in combat. I asked God if there was anything I needed to know, convinced I was going to Hell for my past acts. The poem "Footprints" popped into my mind. God was real...two sets of prints, but at times, only one was visible. God had walked with the writer, but carried him in his darkest times.

I sat thinking of the poem. Was this another revelation? I had actually not read that poem in years, though I thought of it in Kuwait City. Why it popped into my head I had no idea. I like to think it was God carrying me. I finally prayed, "God if you are carrying me now, please don't put me down. Take me where I need to go. I am lost in the dark with no compass."

The next thought came as clear as day. *Go to school.* What would I study? I didn't know anything but the military. *Psychology.* I went home, quit the police force, and started my self-rehabilitation program. I started college, majoring in Psychology. Within five years, I received a Master's Degree in Psychology.

During my studies, I discovered tools to help me cope with my problems. I made a final discovery — one I should have realized a long time before. God is real. He truly loves us; truly loved me, even if it hadn't always been returned. We are his children — some bad, some good. Parents unconditionally love their children. Why would God do any less? That was the key to my happiness. It was hard to find, but so easy to keep.

As life moved forward, a thought continued to occur to me. I couldn't shake the idea that somehow I had cheated death. I couldn't stand it. I joined the Army and went back into the military to give it one more chance. But God must have had a different plan for me. While in the Army, I met and married a woman. I fathered two beautiful boys that I love more than life. After a three year hitch without a scratch, I mustered out of the military for the last time.

A Final Word from the Author

I started writing this book as therapy. I had no intention of publishing it. It was an introverted way of talking about my experiences. Like every person who has ever seen combat, it was not something I wished to share with most people. On the other hand, I felt the general population needed to know what their military endures to ensure their freedom and keep them safe.

I have learned to control the anger I once felt at myself. I learned to trust God. I have even learned to talk about my experiences, and to live day by day. To a select few, I've confessed the urge to take a human life. Don't misinterpret — I would take no pleasure in the suffering of the innocent, but my thoughts are always directed at the evils of society; drug runners, violent criminals, or enemies of foreign lands. Paraphrasing Marine Gunner Sergeant Carlos Hathcock, once you've hunted men, the thought never leaves you. Some wish to forget. For others, the thoughts linger, but they are always there. I have struggled to deal with this for a long time. Finally, I accepted it as a consequence of war. I think of it once in a while, and move on to better thoughts. Once I realized I wasn't alone, the experience of war became easier to accept.

I still remember my friends, but I've learned to accept their deaths. They died in battle, with honor and pride. They died with for their country and their belief in its values as a society of peace, freedom, and happiness. We were common men in uncommon circumstances. It was our job.

Semper Fidelis
Recon 1 — Finger out.

Kuwait

Rescued Children in Hondourous

Iraqi Mine Field

Iraqi Bunker

Kuwait Airport

Kuwait "Cleaning Buildings"

Kuwait

Kuwait "Buring Oil Fields"

Saudi

Fox Hole

Saudi

Hondouran Army

Made in the USA
Coppell, TX
22 December 2021

69904751R00125